At Issue

Do Tax Breaks Benefit the Economy?

Other Books in the At Issue Series:

At Issue

Do Tax Breaks Benefit the Economy?

Amanda Hiber, Book Editor

GREENHAVEN PRESS
A part of Gale, Cengage Learning

GALE
CENGAGE Learning™

Detroit • New York • San Francisco • New Haven, Conn • Waterville, Maine • London

Christine Nasso, *Publisher*
Elizabeth Des Chenes, *Managing Editor*

© 2009 Greenhaven Press, a part of Gale, Cengage Learning.

Gale and Greenhaven Press are registered trademarks used herein under license.

For more information, contact:
Greenhaven Press
27500 Drake Rd.
Farmington Hills, MI 48331-3535
Or you can visit our Internet site at gale.cengage.com

For product information and technology assistance, contact us at

Gale Customer Support, 1-800-877-4253
For permission to use material from this text or product, submit all requests online at
www.cengage.com/permissions

Further permissions questions can be emailed to permissionrequest@cengage.com

Articles in Greenhaven Press anthologies are often edited for length to meet page require-ments. In addition, original titles of these works are changed to clearly present the main thesis and to explicitly indicate the author's opinion. Every effort is made to ensure that Greenhaven Press accurately reflects the original intent of the authors. Every effort has been made to trace the owners of copyrighted material.

Cover image © Images.com/Corbis

LIBRARY OF CONGRESS CATALOGING-IN-PUBLICATION DATA

Do tax breaks benefit the economy? / Amanda Hiber, book editor.
  p. cm. -- (At issue)
  Includes bibliographical references and index.
  ISBN-13: 978-0-7377-4298-5 (hbk.)
  ISBN-13: 978-0-7377-4297-8 (pbk.)
  1. Tax credits--United States--Juvenile literature. 2. Tax incentives--United States--Juvenile literature. 3. Taxation--United States--Juvenile literature. 4. Fis-cal policy--United States--Juvenile literature. 5. United States--Economic policy--Juvenile literature. I. Hiber, Amanda.
  HJ4653.C73D62 2009
  336.24'160973--dc22
                                                              2008053995

Printed in the United States of America
1 2 3 4 5 6 7 13 12 11 10 09

Contents

Introduction

The debate over tax rates is one that has raged through America's history, at least in part because it represents a key distinction between "conservative" and "liberal" politicians. Conservatives tend to favor smaller government, thus favoring lower taxes. These politicians argue that citizens, not the federal government, should have control over how their money is spent. There also is a long-standing conservative argument that lower taxes make for a stronger economy because they encourage greater spending and investment. Liberals, on the other hand, tend to favor bigger government, thus favoring higher taxes. They argue that the government's role is to serve the people, and it provides these services using tax dollars. There is also a notion common among those on the liberal side of the political spectrum that taxes act as an equalizer among citizens on a broad spectrum of wealth.

The tax cuts enacted by two-term President George W. Bush have spurred yet another episode in the debate over the effects of tax rates on the nation's economy. Bush passed one set of tax cuts in 2001 and another in 2003, both of which are set to expire at the end of 2010. By this time, it is projected, these cuts will have saved taxpayers $1.6 trillion. There are many critics, however, who contend that these tax cuts did not benefit *all* taxpayers, but instead they benefited only the wealthy and, in fact, hurt lower- and middle-class Americans. Others argue that while the tax cuts did disproportionately go to wealthier Americans, their benefits have trickled down to all Americans, thereby helping the entire economy. Still others say that even though the tax cuts helped the wealthy more in the short term, in the long term, they hurt all Americans, including the wealthy.

The argument that tax cuts for the wealthy strengthen the economy is based on various premises. In the *Wall Street Jour-*

nal, Stephen J. Entin writes that, "The Bush tax program, particularly the 2003 Tax Act, boosted productivity by encouraging . . . investment." In the same newspaper, Stephen Moore says of Bush's tax cuts, "Once again, tax rate cuts have created a virtuous chain reaction of higher economic growth, more jobs, higher corporate profits, and finally more tax receipts." In other words, overall economic growth and its specific outcomes, such as more jobs, benefit all Americans, whether their tax rates were among those cut, or not. Proponents of President Bush's tax cuts are advocating that they be extended beyond their 2010 deadline, so that their positive effects are not reversed.

Critics of Bush's tax cuts argue that they have negatively affected the economy and Americans in general. A December 13, 2007, *New York Times* editorial goes so far as to say, "The Bush tax cuts, more than any other policy, are crippling the government financially." In *Rolling Stone*, economist and columnist Paul Krugman cites specifics: "In fact, job creation has been much slower under Bush than under [President Bill] Clinton, and overall growth since 2003 is largely the result of the huge housing boom, which has more to do with low interest rates than with taxes." Robert H. Frank writes that "The federal budget deficits created by the recent tax cuts have had serious consequences, even for the wealthy." He cites cuts in funding for scientific research, national security, and road maintenance as examples of places where the deficit has negatively affected all Americans.

The most frequent criticism of Bush's tax cuts is simply that they have shifted the tax burden from those Americans with the most means to those with the least, thus expanding the gulf between wealthy Americans and the less fortunate. In *Mother Jones* magazine, James K. Galbraith writes of the Bush tax cuts, "They benefit a misanthropic plutocracy, transferring tax burdens from the rich to the middle class and from the feds to the states and cities." Krugman writes, "In a recent poll, only a minority of Americans rated the economy as 'excellent' or 'good,' while most consider it no better than 'fair' or 'poor.'" He goes on to explain, "The reason most Americans think the economy is fair to poor is simple: For most Americans, it really is fair to poor. Wages have failed to keep up with rising prices. Even in 2005, a year in which the economy grew quite fast, the income of most non-elderly families lagged behind inflation." Unlike many critics, Krugman agrees that the overall economy has benefited from the tax cuts. But, he says, this economic growth has failed to benefit lower- and middle-class Americans. He writes: "What is happening under Bush is something entirely unprecedented: For the first time in our history, so much growth is being siphoned off to a small, wealthy minority that most Americans are failing to gain ground even during a time of economic growth."

Now that Bush's final term in office has ended, the question of whether or not to extend the tax cuts he pushed through Congress will be dealt with by President Barack Obama. During his presidential campaign, Obama said he "would roll back the Bush tax cuts on the wealthiest Americans back to the level they were under Bill Clinton," while cutting taxes for those earning under about $200,000 per year. As President Obama begins his term in the White House, as the economic growth held up by many as the success of Bush's tax cuts begins to slow, and as more and more economists are using the term "recession" to describe the U.S. economy, the debate over tax breaks is more important now than ever.

1

Tax Incentives for Energy Conservation Would Benefit the Economy

Elias Blawie, Alison Freeman-Gleason, and Todd Glass

Elias Blawie, Alison Freeman-Gleason, and Todd Glass were co-chairs of the energy and clean technology practice of the former international law firm Heller Ehrman.

Companies developing alternative energy technologies have enormous potential. Yet some worry that while there is a market for such development, it will be short-lived, like the Internet and telecommunications boom. To make sure this movement is sustainable, there are issues that must be addressed. Tax incentives for solar and wind energy projects and the like must be made long term, unlike the short-term incentives that have been the norm in recent years. While clean energy industries should eventually be viable without tax incentives, such credits are needed for the initial research and development of these technologies. The United States also needs to invest much more money in this development, as its current investment levels are well below ideal. Lastly, the developers of these new technologies need better intellectual property protection to encourage the sharing of clean technologies globally.

Silicon Valley venture capital [VC] is flowing again, but in a new direction: Energy and clean technologies are the next big thing. In 2006, North American VC investment in the energy and clean technology sector totaled $2.9 billion.

Elias Blawie, Alison Freeman-Gleason, and Todd Glass, "How to Turn Clean Energy into a Powerhouse," *BusinessWeek*, September 6, 2007. Reproduced by permission.

As the cost of energy and concerns about global warming and energy security continue to rise, companies focused on developing clean technologies and alternative power have enormous potential. Energy security and carbon emissions will define the future of energy in the U.S., China, India, the European Union, and most other countries for years to come.

But how sustainable is this industry? One problem is that despite investor enthusiasm, the VC community traditionally looks for rapid returns. Market cycles for newer clean technologies from early development to mass deployment often have longer time frames. And while the world's ever-growing need for energy suggests global market potential, can these technologies be deployed reliably and at a scale large enough for utilities and other large sectors of the economy to adopt and use?

Some suggest that a clean-tech bubble is likely, similar to the boom and bust in alternative energy in the 1970s or the Internet and telecommunications in 2000. In fact, some investors are forming funds to buy distressed properties from ethanol production on the assumption that overinvestment will lead to half-built projects on sale for pennies on the dollar. Also, available investment capital appears to be greater than the number of companies with good technology, experienced teams, and significant market potential.

Make Tax Incentives Long Term

Despite the warning signs in certain sectors, such as ethanol, we see a clear path to developing and sustaining robust markets and businesses in energy and many other clean technologies. But the industry is at an inflection point: Will it gain real traction or end up as another fad and set of buzzwords? If we are to avoid another investment bubble where "carbon footprints" become a forgotten yardstick, we must address several private and public issues.

This industry cannot be built on a system of mercurial tax incentives. Tax incentives that pop up one year, only to disappear the next, do more harm than good. The current federal investment and production tax credits are set to expire at the end of 2008. If they are not extended soon, the development and financing of most solar and wind projects in the U.S. will grind to a halt about halfway through [2009] because such new projects cannot be placed in service before the credits expire. A more effective tax regime would take a longer view, building an incentive window of 5 to 10 years, gradually tapering to create a stable, predictable environment for investment, development, and deployment.

The development of energy technologies that are economically viable independent of tax incentives is paramount. In the long run, these emerging technologies need to be able to compete with conventional technologies in a free market. Within the next 5 to 10 years, wind, solar, and clean coal technologies could become viable and deployed at scale without tax incentives. To reach a scale that cuts costs and makes a difference, the cost and risk associated with clean technologies must become conventional enough that utilities—which are risk-averse and conservative by nature—will own or purchase the output of these new energy facilities.

While there are a healthy number of burgeoning clean-tech companies, if the industry is to thrive, we need to support aggressive research and development of underlying technologies in ways that go beyond the entrepreneurial arena. These include fields from materials sciences and engineering that drive semiconductor and photovoltaic technologies to biological research relevant to producing clean fuel stocks.

Bigger, Bolder Research and Development

The reality is that the money applied to R&D [research and development] is currently well below where it could be. In the past, universities have led the development of technologies that have made the U.S. the leader in technology and innovation, in concert with NASA [National Aeronautics and Space Administration], the National Institutes of Health, and the Defense Advanced Research Projects Agency. Federal funding for basic energy and applied energy research and development has fallen 60% in real dollars from 1978 to 2004.

Clean tech could be a bold new frontier to address one of our most pressing long-term challenges. But the U.S. doesn't support research at anything like the levels necessary to secure a long-term, stable supply of clean, reliable energy that is not dependent on oil from the Middle East. When we reached for the moon in the 1960s, we also laid the foundations for the semiconductor industry and paved the way for advances in computing, telecommunications, and digital imaging. Those efforts have spawned everything from modern microwave ovens to cell phones and digital cameras to many automotive-safety systems that save lives—to the benefit of companies as varied as Intel, Motorola, Eastman Kodak, and TRW Automotive Holdings and their customers, employees, and shareholders. We should make the same commitment to energy-related research if we hope to see similar dividends later this century.

The private and public sectors must come together to realize the enormous potential of clean technology.

The federal government needs to establish a floor for renewable-energy use to provide predictable markets where investors and companies know demand will exist for their products. With these predictable markets and increased demand, capital investment will flow, and all will gain the benefits of decreased costs from larger volumes. So far, more than 20 states have told utilities that a certain percentage of their entire electric power requirements need to come from renewable sources. Among these programs, there is a wide disparity about how such goals are to be met, which leads to risk and ultimately increased costs for utility customers. The U.S. needs to be more forward-thinking. Although it is fair to speculate about its implementation, China's national renewable-energy law, passed in February 2006, is more aggressive in setting mandates for the development and use of renewable energy than any U.S. federal law. The U.S. needs to create a ready market for innovation in renewable energy generation.

Protect Innovators' Ideas

The intellectual-property system for energy technologies should be improved to provide incentives for global deployment of energy technologies by strengthening protections for technology developers. For all their differences, China and the U.S. are inextricably linked in their common energy future. Both countries' efforts to curb climate change, maintain economic growth, and gain energy security depend on coal and low-emissions coal technology. However, without stronger intellectual-property protection, developers of new technologies are dissuaded from licensing or otherwise transferring their technologies to international markets. Instead of locking up new energy technologies, companies could be encouraged by aggressive intellectual-property protections to deploy new clean technologies worldwide.

The most exciting thing about clean tech is the world of opportunity that lies ahead: building new financial markets, solving global climate change and carbon risk, and pioneering the development of new technologies. Now the private and public sectors must come together to realize the enormous potential of clean technology. Success depends on a willingness to make a long-term commitment to the industry as investors, as regulators, and as innovators.

2

Tax Incentives for Energy Conservation Do Not Benefit the Economy

Chris Edwards

Chris Edwards is director of tax policy studies at the Cato Institute. His writings on tax and budget policies have appeared in The Washington Post, Wall Street Journal, Los Angeles Times, *and numerous other publications.*

While tax incentives for energy conservation may reduce energy consumption to some extent, its disadvantages would outweigh any advantages. First, it would further complicate an already convoluted tax code. Such tax credits also would present a wealth of tax incentives that could be used to encourage specific behaviors. Energy conservation should be encouraged in the private sector rather than through tax policy in the public sector. After all, businesses already have significant incentives to decrease their energy consumption. Even if new tax credits are not enacted, energy consumption will fall, due to natural market forces. Congress should not add new tax incentives for energy conservation; however, it should end tax provisions that encourage high energy use. It should also reduce tax penalties against capital investment, which encourage consumption and discourage long-term investing.

Chris Edwards, Testimony before the Senate Committee on Finance, Subcommittee on Energy, Natural Resources, and Infrastructure, Hearing on "Energy Efficiency: Can Tax Incentives Reduce Consumption?" May 24, 2007. Reproduced by permission of The Cato Institute, conveyed through Copyright Clearance Center, Inc.

Additional tax incentives, such as tax credits, probably could reduce U.S. energy consumption modestly. However, narrow incentives complicate the tax code, create distortions that reduce growth, and move down the slippery slope of widespread social engineering through the tax system.

On the other hand, Congress should reform tax provisions that hinder new investments in energy production and conservation. Current business depreciation rules for energy and conservation investments are unfavorable compared to the rules in other countries. Congress should reform those rules, and it should pursue broader tax reforms to spur more rapid replacement of older structures and equipment with newer, more energy efficient infrastructure throughout the economy.

A Breakdown of the Federal Tax System

Policymakers have long considered major reforms to the federal tax system. Some favor a broad-based consumption tax, while others favor a broad-based (or Haig-Simons) income tax. The difference between the two is the treatment of savings and investment. Consumption taxes apply one layer of tax to savings and investment, while income taxes apply two layers. The current federal "income tax" is a hybrid between the two systems.

Reforms to move the current tax code toward a consumption-based system dovetail with the goals of those concerned about America's energy future. A consumption tax would limit current consumption, including energy consumption, while removing tax barriers to investment—including investment in energy production, energy technologies, and energy conservation. As discussed below, more favorable depreciation rules would be an important step in a consumption tax direction.

The federal tax system has become enormously complicated in recent years. The anti-investment bias and high tax rates under the current system have encouraged the proliferation of narrow loopholes and special preferences. There seems to be more interest on Capitol Hill these days in creating new tax credits than in simplifying the tax code to provide fair and equal treatment of all taxpayers.

Opinions of the Past

By contrast, during the 1980s there was bipartisan agreement that the tax code should be reformed to have a broad and neutral base with low rates. One congressional leader on tax reform at the time, Richard Gephardt (D-MO), noted in 1985:

> The main argument for tax reform, I believe, is to achieve greater efficiency in the way the tax code works. When Congress gets into the business of figuring out $370 billion of tax breaks a year, the House Ways and Means Committee and the Senate Finance Committee really are put in the business of trying, at least partially, to plan the American economy.... I confess that I am not qualified to act as a central planner and I do not know anybody on either committee who is.

The Reagan administration held similar views about tax reform. The Congressional Research Service noted that the administration

> opposed using the tax law to promote oil and gas development, energy conservation, or the supply of alternative fuels. The idea was to have a more neutral and less distortionary energy tax policy, which economic theory predicts would make energy markets work more efficiently and generate benefits to the general economy.

The rising number of narrow provisions in the tax code reduces economic efficiency.

The two parties came together and agreed on the landmark Tax Reform Act of 1986, which ended many narrow tax breaks and reduced rates. Unfortunately, "central planning" through the tax code has come back into vogue since then. The number of pages in the federal tax code, regulations, and related rules has increased from 40,500 in 1995 to 67,204 in 2007, an increase of two-thirds.

More Loopholes, Less Efficiency

The number of narrow provisions, or loopholes, in the tax code is rising. . . . The number of tax expenditures for energy jumped from 11 to 23 between 1996 and 2006. The total number of tax expenditures increased from 121 in 1996 to 161 in 2006.

There are problems with these measures of tax expenditures. Some items, such as accelerated depreciation, are counted as loopholes under the income tax. But such pro-investment provisions would not be considered loopholes under a consumption tax. Nonetheless, the OMB's [Office of Management and Budget's] tally of tax expenditures shows that Congress is moving away from the ideal of a neutral tax base toward micromanagement of the economy.

The rising number of narrow provisions in the tax code reduces economic efficiency. Such provisions distort market price and profit signals, which redirects capital and labor into less productive uses. That's why a tax code with a neutral base and low rates is preferable to one with narrow carve-outs and high rates. The economic cost of today's Swiss cheese tax base is large. U.S. output would be substantially higher if the tax base were reformed and effective tax rates across industries were equalized and reduced.

Rising tax code complexity also

- Creates high compliance costs for record keeping, tax filing, and learning tax rules.

- Causes frequent tax filing errors by taxpayers and the Internal Revenue Service [IRS].

- Impedes economic decisionmaking by confusing tax-payers. Many taxpayers do not understand the tax rules for education incentives, retirement savings, and other items.

- Promotes an invasion of privacy by the government. With special breaks, such as those for education and energy, the IRS needs to hunt for volumes of added documentation to carry out its enforcement activities.

Going forward, creating new tax incentives for energy and conservation would exacerbate these complexity problems. New tax incentives would add to the paperwork burden, create more errors in tax administration, further confuse economic decisionmaking, and provide further reason for the IRS to dig into personal affairs.

A Tax Code Manipulated for Social Engineering

Current federal tax incentives for energy and conservation are not large. Total income tax expenditures for these items are valued at just $7 billion in 2007. That represents just 0.3 percent of total federal revenues. Thus, the discussion about tax incentives for energy and conservation is not a discussion about how high federal taxes ought to be.

Instead, the important issue for policymakers is to consider the sort of tax code that America ought to have. Should we have a tax code that treats families and businesses as equally as possible? Or should we have a tax code full of special provisions that treat people differently as Congress micromanages family and business decisions? I favor the former. After all, equality under the law is a bedrock American principle.

Proponents of tax incentives no doubt think that their favored activities deserve special attention. Many energy and environmental analysts argue that federal tax policies should be used to fix "externalities" in energy markets. But such an approach risks opening a Pandora's box of widespread social engineering through the code.

Competitive markets have made a huge contribution toward America's energy security and conservation.

Many interest groups, such as those promoting education, housing, and scientific research, argue that their favored activities are subject to externalities that need special tax code treatment. But, in theory, there are an endless number of externalities that governments could meddle in. At the risk of promoting bad ideas, tax lobbyists could champion tax credits for

- *Obesity.* This is a serious and growing problem that imposes negative externalities on nonobese Americans through the health system and elsewhere. How about a tax credit for membership costs at Gold's Gym?

- *Neighborhood Beautification.* Neat lawns and abundant greenery create positive externalities for neighborhoods. How about a tax credit for tree planting?

- *Guns.* Some analysts say that if more households owned guns it would reduce crime through deterrence. How about a tax credit for gun ownership because of this safety externality?

I'm not advocating these tax credits, but they illustrate the slippery slope of social engineering if Congress wanted to fix every externality through the tax code. [In 2007], the CRS [Congressional Research Service] finds that more than 150 bills on energy efficiency and renewable energy have been introduced, with many proposing narrow tax breaks. I hope Congress resists the temptation to create more tax loopholes.

Conservation and Competitive Markets

The Congressional Research Service noted that the "[Ronald] Reagan administration believed that the responsibility for commercializing conservation and alternative energy technologies rested with the private sector and that high oil prices . . . would be ample encouragement for the development of alternative energy resources." I think Reagan got it right.

Competitive markets have made a huge contribution toward America's energy security and conservation. Businesses, for example, have powerful market incentives to reduce energy consumption. They are relentless in cutting costs—labor costs, tax costs, production costs, fuel costs, heating costs, cooling costs, and lighting costs. Lower costs mean higher profits. That's why businesses strive continually to improve efficiency, including energy efficiency, particularly in today's competitive global economy.

Market forces are behind huge improvements in U.S. energy efficiency in recent decades. The amount of energy consumed for each unit of gross domestic product has fallen dramatically since the 1970s. Economist Gilbert Metcalf found that if U.S. energy intensity were still at the level of 1970, the nation would be consuming 187 quadrillion BTUs [British thermal units] annually. Instead, the United States consumes just 98 quadrillion BTUs annually, and thus we have cut our energy intensity almost in half since 1970.

Some of this improvement stemmed from the changing structure of the U.S. economy. But Metcalf calculates that at least two-thirds of the improvements since 1970 came from rising energy efficiency. And much, perhaps most, of that I think is due to the natural competitive processes in the economy, not government policy.

Consider the rising energy efficiency of household appliances. Federal efficiency standards for appliances went into effect in 1990, and appliance efficiency has improved since then. But appliance efficiency also improved markedly between the early 1970s and 1990, apparently as a market response to rising electricity prices. The average energy consumption of U.S. refrigerators fell from 1,800 kWh [kilowatt hours] per year in 1974 to just 800 kWh by 1990.

If Congress does not change efficiency standards or enact new tax credits for energy conservation, it seems likely that U.S. energy intensity will continue to fall in coming years due to natural market forces.

Congress Can Improve Energy Efficiency

Congress can make tax policy reforms to improve energy efficiency. A first step would be to end any tax provisions that encourage excess energy consumption. A good example are the tax preferences for owner-occupied homes, which some economists think favor the acquisition of particularly large homes. Larger homes need more heating, cooling, and lighting. Thus, one reform would be to combine repeal of the mortgage interest deduction with marginal tax rate cuts.

A new study . . . shows that the current tax code stands in the way of energy and energy efficiency investments.

Another avenue for reform would be to reduce the tax code's bias against capital investment. The income tax encourages current consumption and discourages long-term investment. To fix this bias, Congress should consider more favorable depreciation rules, optimally moving toward immediate expensing of capital purchases. That would remove barriers to all types of investments including those in energy production, alternative fuels, and conservation technologies. The Energy Policy Act of 2005 took some modest steps in this direction, but more could be done.

Policymakers often say that America needs more job-creating investments in computers, automotive plants, transportation, and other activities. Those concerned with energy policy seek greater investment in electricity generation and transmission, oil refining, alternative fuels, pollution control, and conservation technologies. Thus, more favorable tax treatment of capital investment should be a common cause on Capitol Hill.

U.S. Has Few Investment Incentives

A new study by Ernst & Young and the American Council for Capital Formation shows that the current tax code stands in the way of energy and energy efficiency investments. The study compared U.S. cost recovery, or depreciation, rules to the rules in 11 other countries for 11 types of energy investment. Faster write-offs of assets over shorter periods of time reduce effective tax rates on new investment.

The study found that the United States has less favorable tax rules than most other countries for investments in petroleum refining, electricity, pollution control equipment, electricity smart meters, and other items. Here are the results for capital cost recovery after the first five years of an investment:

- Nine of the 11 other countries had more favorable cost recovery for gas and nuclear electricity generation assets than the United States.

- Seven of the 11 other countries had more favorable cost recovery for oil refinery assets.

- Nine of the 11 other countries had more favorable cost recovery for pollution control equipment.

- Ten of the 11 other countries had more favorable cost recovery for electricity smart meters.

Consider electricity smart meters. If a U.S. utility installed these assets, it would take depreciation deductions worth 30 percent of the cost over the first five years. The comparable cost recovery values in other countries are Canada (63 percent), Germany (63 percent), Korea (58 percent), and Malaysia (90 percent).

America's less favorable depreciation rules combined with the industrial world's second-highest corporate tax rate creates a barrier to investment in new and traditional energy technologies. Because Congress is concerned with energy security, conservation, global warming, and high gasoline prices (partly caused by restricted refining capacity), it should focus on removing tax barriers to investment in energy production and energy efficiency.

Congress should consider reinstating the 50 percent capital expensing provisions that were in place in 2003 and 2004. That would spur economic growth while promoting the replacement of all types of older business assets with new, more efficient assets. New machines don't just replace similar old ones, they embody new technologies that increase economic and energy efficiency.

3

Extending Credits to Payroll Taxes Would Be Good for the Economy

Michael Lind

Michael Lind is the Whitehead senior fellow at the New America Foundation. He is the author of several books, including The American Way of Strategy: U.S. Foreign Policy and the American Way of Life.

The Democratic Party needs a popular idea that will win over voters like the Republican tax cuts have done for that party. Allowing all Americans who pay payroll taxes to qualify for every income tax credit would do this. It would extend those credits that are currently available only to those with so much income that they pay both payroll and income taxes to all Americans paying payroll taxes. Such relief is long overdue, considering that the payroll tax has been increased several times since 1980 at the same time that income taxes have been slashed. In effect, the middle class has taken on more and more of the tax burden, while those at higher income levels have taken on less. Extending income tax credits would mean bigger paychecks for the middle class, thus giving the economy a boost by increasing spending. While these extensions would mean a loss in funding for Social Security and Medicare, this could be offset by lifting the cap on payroll taxation, an initiative the American public supports, according to polls. A total tax credit such as this is just the kind of program that American voters would get behind.

The Democrats are a potential majority party in need of a major idea with potential. The major idea that built a Republican majority starting with Ronald Reagan's election was simple: cutting income taxes, with or without cuts in spending. The Republicans reduced income tax rates and then they cut big holes in those rates by creating new or enlarged tax credits available only to Americans who pay income tax.

Meanwhile payroll taxes have risen for working Americans who, because they pay little or no income tax, are ineligible for a range of tax breaks from the $1,000-a-year child tax credit to the home mortgage interest deduction.

Some progressives hope to reverse a generation of Reaganism by repealing George W. Bush's income tax cuts in order to pay for major new spending programs. But the stigma attached to "tax-and-spend" liberalism by a generation of conservative propaganda remains. Equally dubious is the strategy proposed by neoliberal Democrats, whose slogan seems to be: "no pain, no gain." Their formula of budget-balancing fiscal conservatism plus tiny, symbolic subsidies has no popular appeal.

Instead the Democrats should take a leaf from the Republican playbook and position themselves as the party of deep tax cuts for working Americans. What the Reaganites did for affluent income tax payers, Democrats (and like-minded Republicans) can do for America's working-class majority.

Here is a majority-making idea: *Make all Americans who pay payroll taxes eligible for every existing income tax credit— the child tax credit, the home mortgage interest deduction, all of them.* With a single stroke, this would accomplish two important goals. First, it would provide substantial tax relief for working Americans who pay only, or chiefly, payroll taxes. Second, it would permit these same payroll tax payers to enjoy the same tax breaks that more affluent income tax payers now enjoy exclusively.

A Tax Cut for Working Americans

The party that opens up all income tax breaks to all payroll tax payers might be able to consolidate the next majority in American politics, a majority built on center-left, tax-cut Reaganism for the masses, not the elites.

In the past generation, Congress has quietly expanded an invisible welfare state for the well-to-do.

If you're like most Americans, you pay the federal government more money in the form of the 15.3 percent payroll tax taken out of your paycheck every two weeks than you pay in income tax. Even Americans making between $65,000 and $100,000 a year, well above the national median income, pay a greater share of their federal tax dollar for payroll tax than for income tax. You have to be in the highest-earning 20 percent of Americans to pay more income tax than payroll tax.

You'd think that politicians in Washington would be eager to relieve voters of the payroll tax burden, right? Wrong.

Since 1980 the payroll tax has been hiked several times. Meanwhile federal income taxes have been slashed repeatedly—to the benefit, chiefly, of the rich. The wealthiest 5 percent of taxpayers saw their effective federal tax rates fall from 30.1 percent in 2001 to 25.6 percent in 2004, according to the Congressional Budget Office (CBO). And they have benefited even more from steep reductions in taxes on capital gains and dividends.

To make matters worse, more and more of the burden of paying for the federal government has shifted to the payroll tax, which hits middle-class workers the hardest. As a percentage of federal revenue, the payroll tax rose from 27 percent in 1973 to a whopping 40 percent in 2003.

Welfare for the Rich

It gets even worse. In the past generation, Congress has quietly expanded an invisible welfare state for the well-to-do—a generous system of income tax subsidies that is off limits to tens of millions of working-class and middle-class Americans.

Here's how the tax-break welfare state for the affluent works: The IRS [Internal Revenue Service] allows them to take advantage of a number of different tax credits, from the home mortgage interest deduction to the $1,000-a-year child tax credit to a separate credit for money spent by working parents on child care. Under the current tax system, the affluent are also able to shelter large amounts from taxes in tax-preferred savings vehicles like IRAs [Individual Retirement Accounts] and Keogh Plan pensions.

Here's the catch: *You can only claim these tax credits against income taxes, not against payroll taxes.* One-third of American families pay only payroll tax and no income tax. If you belong to one of the families, you're out of luck.

And even if you pay income tax on top of payroll tax, you can only claim these credits for your income tax liability. In theory income tax payers can claim thousands of dollars in total for various deductions—but only if they pay that amount or more in income taxes. The more money you make, the greater your subsidy from the government! Here's one example: In 2005 families earning more than $75,000 saved twice as much money using the child tax credit as families earning less than $30,000.

And we haven't even mentioned corporate income tax breaks that chiefly benefit the economic elite in this country. Hundreds of billions of dollars in potential federal revenues are lost each year because of private company health care plans and pensions—including "gold-plated" plans for corporate executives. If you work for an employer who does not provide either health care or a pension, you're out of luck again.

The Shifting Tax Burden

Reforms in recent decades have created a three-caste society for purposes of taxation. At the bottom, the poor have largely been exempted from taxation and receive such generous tax subsidies as the Earned Income Tax Credit (EITC). At the top, income tax rates have fallen, and the reduced rates, in turn, have been hollowed out by a system of generous tax credits for upper-income households. Stuck in between the affluent and the poor are working-class Americans. They make too much money to receive means-tested subsidies for the poor like the EITC. But they do not qualify for the income-tax welfare state of the affluent because they pay little or no federal income tax. The chief federal tax they pay is the combined Social Security/Medicare payroll tax, for which there are no tax credits comparable to those available to affluent income tax payers.

To put it another way, the United States has moved away from a system of universal social insurance for the broad middle class toward two means-tested welfare states taking the form of tax expenditures and administered by the IRS: a tax-credit welfare state for the poor (the EITC) and another tax-credit welfare state for the affluent.

The idea of granting payroll tax relief has been around since the 1980s. Until now ideas for payroll tax relief have taken four forms: abolition of the payroll tax, permanent payroll tax rate cuts, rebates for payroll taxes, and the extension of the child tax credit to workers who pay payroll tax but not income tax.

To this day the child tax credit is available only to parents who pay income tax.

Al Gore has proposed abolishing the payroll tax and replacing it with a carbon tax. In our book *The Radical Center* (2001), Ted Halstead and I proposed replacing the payroll tax with a progressive consumption tax. There is little political support, however, for completely substituting a new tax for the payroll tax.

In the early 1990s, Senator Daniel Patrick Moynihan proposed permanently cutting payroll taxes so that they met only annual Social Security obligations. Richard Darman, the budget director for President George H.W. Bush, called it "the most irresponsible budget idea of the 1990s." Moynihan's proposal went nowhere in a decade marked by hysteria about the alleged looming bankruptcy of Social Security.

Robert Reich, in this magazine [*The American Prospect*], was just one of a number of writers who floated the idea of payroll tax rebates in the early 2000s, as part of efforts to devise a progressive alternative to the further round of income tax cuts proposed by the current President [George W.] Bush and enacted by the Republican Congress. Like proposals for the abolition of payroll taxes and Moynihan's proposed rate cuts, the rebate proposals would help many working Americans. But all three kinds of proposed reforms are completely unconnected to the question of income tax expenditures, which would continue to exist and continue to be unavailable to payroll tax payers.

An Idea with Conservative Origins

The link between income tax credits and the payroll tax was actually made by Newt Gingrich and his Republican colleagues in the 1994 Contract with America. The Contract proposed extending the then-novel child tax credit to working parents who paid payroll taxes but not income taxes. Once in power, the Republicans reneged on their promise, and to this day the child tax credit is available only to parents who pay income tax. But the idea did not die. It was recently revived by the Center for American Progress, which has proposed making the child tax credit refundable to all families who pay payroll taxes.

This is an excellent idea—but why limit the reform to only one tax credit? Here is a simple, bold, and elegant proposal which at one stroke would universalize the income tax credit system and, at the same time, grant significant payroll tax relief to stressed American households: *Make all Americans who pay payroll taxes eligible for all existing income tax credits for children, housing, education, savings, and other purposes.* Every single tax credit that can now be claimed by individual income tax payers, from the child tax credit to the home mortgage interest deduction, should be available to all Americans who pay the payroll tax. Every single one. No exceptions.

Call it the Total Tax Credit (TTC) system. Under the TTC system, even if you don't pay income taxes, your employer would let you deduct your tax credits from the payroll tax that is sent to the government every two weeks. Result: fatter biweekly paychecks for all American workers. The biggest winners would be those who could claim the most TTC deductions: home-owning families with dependent children. But even single, childless renters who don't pay income tax, or pay only a small amount, could benefit as well—for example, from tax credits for savings. In this way, today's tax credit system exclusively for income tax payers would be turned overnight from a professional-class gated community into a mainstream middle-class neighborhood.

But wait. Wouldn't allowing payroll tax payers to claim credits against the payroll tax blow a huge hole in revenues? Wouldn't we need to make up for the lost revenue in order to fund Social Security and Medicare? Of course we would. And we could, in various ways.

The first step would be to lift the cap on payroll taxation, which is now $97,500 a year. The American public supports the idea of lifting the cap on Social Security payroll taxes. In a February 2005 *Washington Post* poll, 81 percent said that Americans who make more than the present limit should pay Social Security tax on their wage income. There is a precedent for this long-overdue reform: In 1993 Congress removed the similar cap that previously existed on Medicare taxes on wage income.

Would lifting the cap hurt mainstream Americans? Hardly. Only the top 5 percent or 6 percent of wage earners would see their Social Security tax go up. These are the same people who have received most of the benefits from tax cuts over the past 30 years. They can afford it.

The Total Tax Credit system would . . . affect the economy indirectly, to the benefit of the broad middle class.

Lifting the cap while keeping benefits for affluent retirees unchanged would produce a surplus for Social Security for the next 75 years. But this assumes no payroll tax relief for middle-income workers. If we adopt the Total Tax Credit system, then the money that streams in from applying payroll taxation to wage income higher than $97,500 would fill part of the revenue shortfall created by extending income tax credits to payroll tax payers. But we would still need to cut spending elsewhere or come up with new revenues.

Additional Benefits

How about imposing a cap on tax expenditures—while lifting the cap on payroll tax? Right now the benefits of the home mortgage deduction go disproportionately to the richest Americans with the biggest houses. Capping the home mortgage interest deduction at, say, the median amount spent by homeowners would result in new revenue flowing from the rich into federal coffers—*without raising existing federal income tax rates at all*. Politically speaking it's much more attractive to raise revenue by capping income tax loopholes than to raise income tax rates. Reducing the amount of money the wealthy can shelter in tax-favored savings vehicles alone would result in a flood of new revenues to the Treasury. The price of extending today's income-tax-only credits to all American payroll tax payers without bankrupting the government may be to make all tax credits—for housing, children, and education—more modest. But that's how it should be, anyway.

The Total Tax Credit system would also affect the economy indirectly, to the benefit of the broad middle class. As take-home pay for working people increased, the economy's spending on housing, day care, and other sectors would come to include the less affluent. A universalized home mortgage interest deduction capped below the current $1 million would encourage realtors to build a greater number of modest homes, rather than second homes and McMansions. Day-care centers would find a new clientele in working-class parents as well as professionals. Allowing payroll tax payers to cut their payroll tax by saving money in tax-favored retirement accounts would create an entirely new source of capital for banks. America's tax-credit-subsidized economy would shift downmarket—and about time, too.

If Necessary, Raise Taxes on Luxuries

Lifting the cap on payroll taxes while capping the newly universal tax credits might still result in revenue shortfalls. We could increase other taxes that fall lightly on working people, such as income taxes, taxes on capital gains and dividends, and estate taxes. Or we could raise revenue from new taxes, like a national sales tax or value-added tax (VAT) on luxury goods. Think about it—a national tax on luxuries enjoyed by the wealthy could help to pay the cost of extending tax breaks now enjoyed by elite income tax payers to ordinary payroll tax payers.

But our representatives should prefer to raise new revenue to pay for the Total Tax Credit system by means of consumption taxation rather than higher income taxes, and the reason is political, not economic. Consumption taxes, like national VATs elsewhere in the world, state and local sales taxes in the

United States, and, for that matter, payroll taxes, have the political advantages of being inescapable and invisible. Payroll and consumption taxes are difficult if not impossible to avoid. And even more importantly, because they are relatively invisible compared to highly transparent taxes like the income tax and property tax, consumption taxes and payroll taxes are less likely to provoke tax revolts.

In Europe the architects of generous social-insurance systems have been wise to rely heavily on non-transparent taxes like payroll taxes and consumption taxes. While these are regressive, in Europe their effect has been moderated by progressive spending. In the taxophobic United States, we could achieve the same result by making our tax burden more progressive. Social-democratic purists may lament the fact that so much public policy in the United States is done via the tax code rather than direct spending programs. But instead of complaining that the United States is not Sweden, American progressives and centrists ought to make a virtue of necessity and make the existing tax-expenditure welfare state nearly universal (by allowing payroll tax payers to participate) and more progressive (by capping the new federal total tax expenditures). . . .

The TTC Would Not Discriminate

Conservatives have had considerable success in arguing against making income tax credits refundable for the non-tax-paying poor. They argue that the very concept of "tax expenditures," which treats special-purpose tax breaks like the child tax credit as the equivalent of government spending, is an academic fiction. In reality, they argue, these tax breaks are not government subsidies at all. The government is simply allowing taxpayers to keep more of their own money.

But this argument against extending income tax credits to Americans with little or no tax liability does not work against extending income tax credits to Americans with another kind of tax liability—payroll tax liability. Conservatives may argue that the untaxed poor don't deserve tax breaks—but working-class Americans are taxpayers themselves. Conservatives cannot argue that Americans who pay payroll tax should be discriminated against in favor of Americans who pay income tax. Doing so would be political suicide.

How could conservatives possibly object to cutting taxes and modifying existing programs to make them more fair?

In an ideal world, the Total Tax Credit would be refundable so that non-taxpayers among the working poor would get them, too, in the form of federal subsidies like the EITC. However, abandoning the goal of making the Total Tax Credit refundable to the non-tax-paying poor might be the price of a bipartisan coalition to enact this important reform.

Besides, Republicans who oppose the TTC will doubtless have it pointed out to them it was Newt Gingrich who in 1994 proposed making the child tax credit available to payroll tax payers—a key element of the Total Tax Credit proposal. And it was Bush who in 2006 proposed capping "gold-plated" income tax expenditures, a precedent for another key element of the TTC system: capping "gold-plated" tax expenditures that benefit the affluent.

"Lift, Cap, and Share"

Nor would the TTC pit income tax payers against payroll tax payers. On the contrary, large numbers of income tax payers would be able to add their payroll tax to their income tax, against which they could claim bigger tax credits. Many in the upper-middle class as well the lower-middle and working classes would benefit from a Total Tax Credit law.

Making payroll tax payers eligible for all income tax credits is a big idea that can shake up the stagnant domestic policy debate. We've had three decades of income tax cuts for the elites; now it's time for payroll tax cuts for the masses. "Lift, cap, and share" should be the motto of proponents of the TTC system. Lift the cap on payroll taxation; cap all income tax expenditures; and share all existing income tax expenditures with Americans who pay payroll tax, even if they pay no income tax at all. If Democrats are shrewd enough to take up this cause, they could immunize themselves against conventional right-wing attacks. How could conservatives possibly object to cutting taxes and modifying existing programs to make them more fair? (There would still be the option of adding new tax credits in the future, like one to help people buy health insurance under an individual mandate system or to offset public health programs paid for by state taxes.)

It's time to share the credit—the tax credit. The next president should work with Congress to ensure that all taxpayers get exactly the same tax breaks, whether they pay income tax on top of payroll tax or payroll tax alone. That's not only fair—it's the American thing to do.

4

Family Tax Credits Are Not Good for the Economy

Shawn Macomber

Shawn Macomber is a contributing editor at The American Spectator. *His work has also appeared in* The Wall Street Journal, The Weekly Standard, Reason, *and other publications.*

While Bill Clinton supposedly ended the welfare system in the U.S. during his presidency, Democrats continue to sell some version of it, using conservative rhetoric. They promote the redistribution of wealth, as usual, and call it "tax cuts" for the working class. One way they seek to implement these is through expansion of family tax credits. However, these credits do not currently work in accordance with their original intent; moreover, they often result in refunds for Americans who pay no taxes in the first place. Family tax credits, including the child tax credit, are difficult to argue against politically, and conservatives' unwillingness to oppose them has only made the Democratic case stronger. Politicians of both parties need to acknowledge that the family tax credits amount to another form of welfare.

In George Orwell's *1984*, the authoritarian rulers of Oceania evaded the general population's distaste for certain policies by simply "eliminating undesirable words" and "stripping such words as remained of unorthodox meanings, and so far as possible of all secondary meanings whatever." The language left was "deliberately constructed for political purposes: words, that is to say, which not only had in every case a political im-

Shawn Macomber, "Tax Credit Welfare," *The American Spectator*, vol. 38, April 2005, pp. 40–41. Copyright © 2005 The American Spectator. Reproduced by permission.

plication, but were intended to impose a desirable mental attitude upon the person using them."

Put another way, change the word and you change the debate. This tactic has been on display in recent years during the welfare debate. More than a decade ago, President Bill Clinton and Congress came together "to end welfare as we know it." It's an achievement Democrats have not stopped braying over ever since, although it clearly was more the brainchild of Newt Gingrich [Republican Speaker of the House of Representatives from 1995 to 1999] than Bill Clinton.

Yet the core philosophies that drove a failed and unpopular social experiment in the first place were never abandoned. They were just cloaked in "new-speak." The statist elements of the government simply eliminated the offending words and continued the long march towards the Utopian collective, the founding principle of which has always been and shall always remain the redistribution of wealth.

Consider: Despite the utter failure of (still just a) Senator John Kerry's apocalyptic campaign rhetoric about "tax cuts for the wealthy," Democrats have been unwilling to drop the language of class warfare. Senate Minority Leader Harry Reid, House Minority Leader Nancy Pelosi, recently elected [February 12, 2005] DNC [Democratic National Committee] Chair Howard Dean, and John Edwards [Democratic senator from 1999 to 2005] have all continued to recite the mantra of rich vs. poor with a religiosity that is completely out of character.

On the face of things such rhetoric seems ineffective. Democrats hold an advantage in most polls vis-a-vis public perception of which party is fighting for the working class, but it isn't working for them in terms of obtaining and expanding real political power. The "Two Americas" speech did not carry the day for Edwards in the primaries. Kerry's campaign trail claim that "the burden of taxes has shifted from the wealthy to the middle class" did not deliver the November [2004] election.

New Spin on an Old Idea

Class warfare, however, still sells. It has just been adapted to the times, gradually morphing into a more virulent strain. Democrats and liberal Republicans have no intention of supporting "welfare" again. Instead they have adopted the successful rhetoric of devotees of limited government, and used it for the exact opposite purpose. Now they argue in self-righteous tones for "tax cuts for the working class"—in other words, tax cuts for people who don't pay taxes. These large returns have essentially become government subsidies to individuals or welfare recipients, laundered through the one organization few in Washington, DC, dare confront—the Internal Revenue Service [IRS].

This redistribution of wealth is run under the auspices of "family tax credits" that are named in such a way that no politician planning to seek re-election would ever dare publicly question. It is one thing to complain about "welfare queens," but quite another thing altogether to argue against the Child Tax Credit.

It's a trend that is accelerating. In 2002, for example, the IRS sent out a combined $58 billion in "tax refunds" to families through the Earned Income Tax Credit (EITC) and Child Tax Credit (CTC) programs. That same year the federal government spent only $21 billion on traditional welfare services.

This was not how these programs were intended to function. The EITC was enacted in 1975 and remained a very small program doling out a couple hundred dollars to offset Social Security taxes for the poor, before suddenly skyrocketing into the thousands in the early '90s. Likewise, the CTC started off in the mid-'90s as a $400 credit, before jumping up to $1,000 as part of the congressional deal to make President [George W.] Bush's first term tax cuts a reality. The percentage recipients can receive in cash over and above their tax liability was also increased from 10 to 15 percent during those negotiations.

Should Nontaxpayers Get Refunds?

Here's how it works: If Jane, a single mother with one dependent child, earned $17,000 last year and owes $200 in taxes, her $1,000 CTC eliminates all of her tax liability with $800 left over. Since 15 percent of her income over $10,750 is more than the remainder of her tax credit ($938/$800), she takes home the $800 as a "refund." This is combined with an EITC of $2,120 for a total refund of $2,920 to a taxpayer who paid in zero tax dollars.

Here's another wholly fictional case run through the official IRS "refund" calculators: John and Joanne, a married couple with three children, earned a combined total of $29,000 last year. Through various standard deductions, the couple's tax bill begins at zero. They can claim a CTC of $3,000, but only take home the lesser amount of 15 percent of their income over $10,750, which is $2,738. The couple's EITC is $1,350 for a grand total of $4,088. Not only is that a $4,088 government subsidy for John and Joanne, it's also the rough equivalent of a 14 percent pay raise for 2004.

Enough of these charades! Either we are still in the business of welfare, or we are not.

Conservative eagerness to surrender when debate over family tax credits comes up has only emboldened the opposition to push harder. Shortly after the announcement that the CTC would remain at $1,000 for 2004 instead of dropping to $700 as planned, the liberal advocacy group Citizens for Tax Justice issued a dire press release headlined, "Bush Tax Plan's Child Credit Boost Leaves Behind One in Four of America's Children." Even with an increase, protesters still showed up at the White House pushing symbolic baby strollers. Some liberal think tanks began advocating free tax return consultations for "the poor" (almost everyone is poor in their books) to make sure they got every government dollar coming to them.

Few Republicans Voice Opposition

While conservatives such as Americans for Tax Reform's Grover Norquist and the Cato Institute's Doug Bandow have appropriately questioned the logic of "tax cuts" for people who do not pay taxes, Republican politicians have heartily embraced the idea and even attempted to claim it as their own. For example, one Bush/Cheney television spot during the 2004 campaign intoned that John Kerry "opposed increasing the child tax credit 18 times." The ad was in effect criticizing the Massachusetts senator for not being a big enough booster of the welfare state.

It is ironic that Bush and Kerry campaigned as scions of fiscal responsibility while both simultaneously endorsed a plan that "refunds" billions upon billions of dollars to non-taxpayers.

Republican senators Chuck Grassley and Olympia Snowe have gone even further, demanding that the IRS seek out those families that don't take advantage of these credits.

"The IRS forgot the 'service' part of its name and mission," Grassley said, adding, "It's a waste to have tax credits a lot of people miss. This makes me wonder how many other tax breaks low-income taxpayers qualify for but don't claim because they aren't aware of them. The IRS needs to do a lot better job of spotting oversights in the taxpayers' favor."

Proponents of family tax credits often wax philosophical about the "moral imperative" of providing such "relief." Enough of these charades! Either we are still in the business of welfare, or we are not. If the only way the forces of Big Government statism can win the debate is with a smoke and mirror campaign of "newspeak" and artful dodges, perhaps it is time they face a real opposition, rather than a conservative movement that fought welfare to the death only to bow before flowery language and innuendo.

5

Tax Breaks for Hedge Fund Managers Do Not Benefit the Economy

Randall Dodd

Randall Dodd is president of the Financial Policy Forum, which researches and recommends policy on market oversight and regulation. He has a Ph.D. in economics from Columbia University.

In the past, when hedge funds and private equity firms were small and did not raise a lot of capital, they were made exempt from regulation. But this status is now outdated, as these firms and their profits have grown enormous. They are also allowed tax breaks that are inappropriate, given their size and power. For instance, managers of these firms can treat a large portion of their compensation as capital gains rather than as salary. These special tax provisions give tax breaks to some of the least deserving members of society. Not only are hedge fund managers some of the wealthiest taxpayers, they also have a substantial record of white-collar crime. Claims that treating hedge funds like other income would threaten the pensions of working Americans and increase the costs of consumer goods and services are simply untrue. Analysis by market research firms shows that these tax loopholes cost the U.S. Treasury $6.3 billion a year. This is money that could be much better spent.

Randall Dodd, "Tax Breaks for Billionaires," *Economic Policy Institute Policy Memorandum*, No. 120, July 24, 2007. Copyright © 2007 Economic Policy Institute. Reproduced by permission.

Private investment companies, organized as hedge funds or private equity firms, have recently grown into major economic forces in the U.S. economy. They mobilize capital, and often leverage it with borrowed funds, in order to accumulate a tremendous amount of assets under their management. These investments include leveraged buyouts; market-neutral investment strategies in publicly traded stocks and bonds, energy, and other commodities; various arbitrage [buying and selling] strategies; as well as many lesser known and some entirely unreported transactions. Hedge funds are big players in the large corporate take-over activity that reached $3.6 trillion in 2006, and they are also responsible for a significant share of trading volume on the major stock exchanges and in some over-the-counter derivatives markets.

These private pools of capital are unregulated, or exempt from Securities and Exchange Commission (SEC) regulation, under both the Investment Advisors Act and the Investment Company Act. While these exemptions were once justified on the grounds that such investment firms were small, closely held, and did not raise their capital in public capital markets, the exemptions are no longer consistent with today's reality. Today these firms are huge, have a wide number and range of investors, and the Internet has blurred the distinction between public and private marketing.

These super-rich fund managers do not need and certainly do not deserve special tax breaks.

In addition to being unregulated, these financial institutions also reap substantial benefits from special tax provisions that, like the regulatory framework, are no longer appropriate. The professional fund managers of these hedge funds and private equity firms are allowed to treat a substantial portion of their compensation as capital gains, meaning they are most likely taxed at 15% rather than the 35% rate that applies to ordinary income such as wages and salary. Such an exemption, however, makes little sense: in economic terms, the fund managers (also known as investment advisors) perform a professional service, much like lawyers or doctors, and receive remuneration for their labor.

Faulty Loophole

These investment advisors and hedge fund managers can take advantage of this tax structure because they are often compensated through a scheme that, in part, pays them according to the returns on the fund. The industry standard for hedge fund managers is "two and twenty," which is shorthand for an "overhead" fee of 2% of capital under management plus carried interest (often called a "carry") of 20% of the returns on the fund. Thus a $100 million fund earning 20% would pay its fund manager $2 million for overhead and $4 million in carry. The carry portion of their compensation is treated under the tax code as capital gains for the fund manager and is taxable at the much lower capital gains tax rate of 15%. . . .

There are two things economically wrong with this special tax provision for hedge fund managers. First is its impact on *economic efficiency*. It creates inconsistent economic incentives (i.e., distortions) for some labor income to be treated as ordinary income while other labor income is treated as capital gains, and the work done by investment advisors is undeniably a professional, laboring activity. Fund managers at pension funds, trusts, and endowments who provide similar professional services are paid a salary and possibly a bonus, and these are all treated as ordinary income. Only because hedge funds and private equity firms are organized as limited liability partnerships—which are already treated favorably for tax and liability purposes—are these same professional services taxed differently. The result is a distortion in the compensation and after-tax income between these super-rich hedge fund managers and millions of others in the workforce.

The second thing wrong with this exemption is that these super-rich fund managers do not need and certainly do not deserve special tax breaks. *Alpha Magazine* reports the compensation for hedge fund managers each year. The top earner for 2006 received $1.7 billion, the second highest received $1.4 billion, and the third $1.3 billion. That adds to $4.4 billion for three people. The top 25 hedge managers received, on average, $570 million for a total of $14.25 billion....

More Harm than Good

Not only do these rich individuals have no need of tax breaks, the hedge fund and private equity industries have demonstrated time and again that they are not exemplary economic citizens who deserve privileged tax treatment. While most fund managers are probably law-abiding investment advisors, there are innumerable examples of wrong doing. The major types of failures and illegal activities include insider trading, IPO [initial public offering] manipulation, embezzlement, and defrauding mutual fund investors.

> *The loss to the U.S. Treasury ... amounts to at least $6.3 billion a year.*

Defending this tax break are highly paid lobbyists such as Douglas Lowenstein and Grover Norquist who loudly and repeatedly make the claim that taxing hedge fund managers like everyone else will harm the average working family. They claim that taxing hedge funds like normal income will harm pension fund returns. This is wrong on two levels. First, the tax change would apply to hedge fund managers and not investors (many pension funds invest in hedge funds). Second, pension funds do not pay taxes. These lobbyists also claim that it would increase the cost of consumer goods and services because so many stores and chain restaurants are owned by private equity firms and hedge funds. This, too, is preposterous because, again, the tax does not apply to the investors or owners of those businesses but only the investment advisors who manage the funds of those investors. Moreover, the businesses owned by private pools of capital will have to compete with other similar businesses providing consumer goods and services—only now on a level playing field—and they will not be able to arbitrarily raise their prices.

The Revenue Costs

How much revenue does this loophole cost the federal government? The following analysis creates a reasonable estimate using what information is available from the unregulated, non-transparent hedge fund industry.

The data come from market research firms Greenwich Associates and HedgeFund.net. These firms study the industry in order to help investors become more informed about the size, returns, and range of opportunities available in the area of professionally managed private capital pools. The size of the hedge fund industry is best measured by the amount of capital invested in these funds. HedgeFund.net estimates what is called "assets under advisement" to be $2.4 trillion for 2006. Greenwich Associates regularly reports on its survey of a large number of fund managers, and the results . . . [since 2003] show that hedge fund investments' across-the-board investment strategies returned 10.5% to investors after fees. This implies that returns were 13.1% before fees, and if investment managers received the industry standard 20%, then their remuneration treated as "carry" was $63 billion for 2006 (20% of returns calculated as rate of return times capital of $2.4 trillion).

Of course not all hedge funds are located in the United States, but estimates are that 70% of hedge funds measured by capital invested are based domestically. The funds may also have subsidiaries in the Cayman Islands for certain other tax purposes, but the fund managers are taxed based on where they live, and most live in the United States. If we take a more conservative estimate that 50% of hedge fund assets under advisement are managed by advisors located in the United States, then half of those investment advisory earnings are taxable under U.S. law. At the current 15% capital gains tax rate, the taxable amount would result in $4.75 billion in tax payments; at the top rate (35%) on ordinary income, it would sum to $11.05 billion. The loss to the U.S. Treasury, therefore, amounts to at least $6.3 billion a year.

Congress has the opportunity to correct a bad economic policy and free up resources to fund better priorities.

Money Not Well Spent

In addition to these aggregate numbers, there are a few specific figures coming out of the private capital market worth considering. *Alpha Magazine*'s figures for the top hedge fund managers and its estimates of the break out of compensation between salary and bonus can be used to further estimate the revenue implication by applying that break out to the portion of total compensation that is likely treated as capital gains. The different tax rates then can be used to calculate how much these three individuals benefit from this quirk in the tax law.

A simple calculation shows that this preferential tax treatment for the top 25 individuals alone costs the Treasury almost $2 billion. It serves to suggest that our estimates of tax losses are indeed conservative, as the losses from these 25 managers alone amounts to almost a third of our total.

Congress has the opportunity to correct a bad economic policy and free up resources to fund better priorities. This analysis points to the need to update the nation's tax laws dealing with private pools of capital. The current law is generating inefficiencies and great inequality by granting tax breaks to individuals who do not need and do not deserve such favors. The nation has greater and more deserving priorities. If the amount of tax revenue lost to private equity firm managers is equivalent to that lost with hedge funds, then the combined amount would be $12.6 billion. This forgone revenue stream could, for example, fully fund the five-year, $35 billion expansion of SCHIP [State Children's Health Insurance Program], the public health insurance program for low-income children.

6

Additional Housing Tax Credits Would Not Benefit the Economy

Gerald Prante

Gerald Prante is a senior economist at the Tax Foundation, where he focuses on federal income tax and state and local property tax issues. He is currently a Ph.D. student in economics at George Mason University.

Congress is currently considering yet another housing tax credit, this one proposed by Senators Debbie Stabenow and Johnny Isakson. This credit, allegedly intended to help the struggling housing market, would provide a temporary tax break for buying a home. First of all, there are already too many housing tax credits in the current tax code. These credits violate one of the basic principles of sound tax policy, which is to keep people from making financial decisions based solely on the tax code. They also encourage investment in housing over investment in business and may even make the current housing crisis worse. The proposed credit is bound to be factored into the selling price of a home, thereby distorting home prices. Finally, such a tax credit will need to be paid for somehow. Instead of being good for the economy, this tax credit is simply another handout for homeowners and the housing industry that its supporters can sell as a tax cut.

Today Democrats and Republicans in Congress are considering yet another special tax incentive for housing as a response to the current crisis in the housing sector. Bipartisan though it may be, no current tax idea is more counterproductive.

The *Wall Street Journal* reported on Saturday, March 22 [2008] that Sens. Debbie Stabenow (D-MI) and Johnny Isakson (R-GA) have floated proposals on Capitol Hill to create a temporary tax credit for buying a home, hoping to prop up the flagging housing market.

Sen. Isakson proposes a $5,000 tax credit that could be claimed by homebuyers in three circumstances: (1) the house is vacant; (2) the house is occupied by an owner in default on his mortgage; or (3) the house has been foreclosed on. The non-refundable credit could be claimed for three consecutive years and total as much as $15,000. Sen. Stabenow's refundable, one-year credit has different strings attached. It would be limited to first-time homebuyers who, if filing a joint return, could claim $6,000 or 10 percent of the home price, whichever is lower. Note that both of these provisions are credits that allow people to subtract that amount directly from their final tax bill, saving them much more money than deductions from taxable income like the mortgage interest deduction.

The tax code is already littered with special tax provisions that favor housing, and public finance economists all along the political spectrum agree that they are excessive, to say the least. From the mortgage interest deduction to the deduction for real estate taxes paid to the capital gains exclusion for primary residences, the federal tax code funnels more than $100 billion dollars annually into the housing sector. That's nearly 10 percent of total federal income tax collections, enough so that if the subsidies were repealed, we could cut every personal income tax rate by 14 percent. And that's without counting the billions spent directly by the Department of Housing and Urban Development (HUD) and the government-created entities known as Freddie Mac and Fannie Mae.

The large, temporary credits offered by Sens. Isakson and Stabenow would make . . . [the housing crisis] worse.

The Mortgage Interest Deduction

Most sacrosanct among all these subsidies is the mortgage interest deduction, advertised by real estate agents, homebuilders and other special interests as if it were Mom's apple pie. Of course, interest payments on loans taken out to earn taxable income should be deductible, and those payments have been deductible since the income tax was born in 1913. But mortgage loans taken out by homeowners on their primary residences are not used to produce taxable income, so mortgage interest should not be deductible.

The President's Tax Reform Panel recommended in 2005 that the home mortgage deduction be scaled back and rechanneled to taxpayers with lower incomes. It recommended repealing the property tax deduction in its entirety. Importantly, these changes proposed by the Tax Reform Panel exchanged some of the housing tax subsidies for lower tax rates overall.

The objective of most sound tax policy is for the tax code to interfere with household and business decisions as little as possible—that is, to let decisions be made on economic fundamentals, not based on their tax treatment. Housing tax subsidies have violated this tenet of sound tax policy and distorted household decisions in several important ways. First, they encourage investment in housing over investment elsewhere in the economy, namely business investment. Secondly—and this is something that should be appreciated more right now—the deductions for mortgage interest and real estate taxes paid grow with the size of the house and the mortgage, encouraging the financing of oversized houses with oversized loans. It would go too far to blame the current housing crisis on the existing tax subsidies, but they certainly haven't helped matters. Similarly, the large, temporary credits offered by Sens. Isakson and Stabenow would make matters worse.

Why Hurt Business Investment to Favor Housing Investment?

Recently, the U.S. Treasury Department calculated that economy-wide, the effective tax rate on new investment is 17.3 percent. However, the same study calculated an effective tax rate on investment in residential housing of only 3.5 percent. In other words, housing already receives very special tax treatment compared to other types of investment.

Every year the federal government preserves these tax advantages for housing investment, it must continue to impose higher income tax rates on other people and industries. If either the Isakson or Stabenow credit were to be piled on top of the existing credits, the only way to prevent further tax hikes on other people and industries would be to cut government spending at the same time. We know how unlikely that is.

This credit . . . would increase investment in housing at the expense of other investment, which will help our economy far less than an across-the-board tax cut would.

The usual rationalization for giving housing investment a substantial preference is that spillover benefits, or "positive externalities," flow from homeownership. Lower crime is one that's frequently cited. Under this justification, there is no "distortion" from housing subsidies, but rather a positive market correction that admittedly tilts investment toward housing, but for good reason. Realistically, however, there is no plausible proof that the glow of homeownership is so beneficial to the rest of society that it's worth such a mammoth subsidy in its current or proposed form.

If permanent tax credits have in any way helped push people into subprime mortgages in recent years—and there is every reason to think they have abetted that process—would the same thing happen with temporary credits such as those offered by Stabenow and Isakson?

Effect on Home Prices

Any tax credit, permanent or temporary, will to some extent be capitalized into the price of housing. In other words, sellers can and will charge more for a house if they know the buyer will be getting a tax credit. From the homebuyer's perspective, he might be willing to pay more, knowing that he'll be getting the amount of the credit refunded to him when he files his tax return. How much of the credit will be captured by the seller, propping up the price of housing, and how much will be captured by the buyer, boosting home purchases?

If the tax subsidy of the Isakson or Stabenow credits were *fully* capitalized into the price, then the seller—a homebuilder if the house is new and a homeowner if it isn't—would capture the entire value of the credit. In the case of the Isakson proposal, every potential buyer of a qualified home would be eligible, so the seller might be expected to capture close to the full $15,000 value of the credit. With Stabenow's credit, only first-time buyers would be eligible, and the credit's value would double for married couples. So every seller's ideal customer would be that couple who qualifies for the maximum tax credit of $6,000 and could therefore pay that much more for the home. The next best buyer would be a single person buying his first home, permitting the seller to try to extract an additional $3,000 from the buyer. Other buyers would not qualify for the credit and would therefore be less willing to match the prices offered by first-time buyers. In each case, if this capitalization occurs, the credit would accomplish little to make homes easier to buy because the seller would be capturing a large fraction of the credit.

More realistically, the tax credit would be *partially* capitalized into the price of the home, thereby increasing the prices somewhat but also increasing investment into housing by some amount. Therefore, the distortion created by this credit would be twofold. First, it would increase investment in housing at the expense of other investment, which will help our economy far less than an across-the-board tax cut would. Secondly, any politically targeted tax cut like Isakson's or Stabenow's forces taxes to be higher somewhere else, forces spending to be cut, and/or causes the deficit to increase (i.e. future taxes to increase).

Just Another Handout

Overall, while a housing tax credit by itself might increase investment in that sector, there is no free lunch here. Like any spending program, a tax credit for housing must be paid for.

And that brings us to an interesting question: What is the difference between subsidies delivered through the tax code, like the new tax credits proposed by Isakson and Stabenow, and the spending programs of HUD? In principle, there's no difference. It's just that one can be called a "tax cut" by its supporters while the other can be criticized as a big spending program. In reality, allowing homeowners to take an additional $5,000 or more off their tax bills is a handout to homeowners and those in the housing industry.

If the proposed credits put forth by Sens. Isakson and Stabenow were accompanied by elimination of the deduction for real estate taxes paid and a scaling back of the mortgage interest deduction, as recommended by the Tax Reform Panel, they would dramatically improve the federal tax code. But, as Senator Obama did with his housing tax credit proposal, Isakson and Stabenow want to pile new credits on top of the excessive tax subsidies that the housing market already receives.

Ideally, American political leaders would actually explain to the people why the government should be pushing renters to buy houses they may not be able to afford instead of continuing to rent.

Unfortunately, as with much of tax policy in Washington, short-run political interests, the tyranny of the status quo, and heavy influence from special interests prevent a true discussion of what tax policy should be.

7

Making Tax Credits Refundable Would Benefit the Economy

Fred T. Goldberg Jr., Lily L. Batchelder, and Peter R. Orszag

Fred T. Goldberg Jr. is a tax attorney who served as commissioner for the Internal Revenue Service from 1989 to 1992. Lily L. Batchelder is assistant professor of Law and Public Policy at New York University; her research focuses on the relationship between taxation and social policy. Peter R. Orszag, an economist, is the current director of the U.S. Congressional Budget Office.

Tax incentives currently reduce federal tax revenues by about $500 billion a year, most of which comes in the form of deductions, exemptions, or exclusions. These incentives are frequently tied to a filer's tax bracket, though, so that they do not reach a large portion of Americans whose incomes are so low that they owe very little, or no, federal income tax. Making tax credits refundable would provide the same tax benefits to all filers, even those who do not owe income taxes. Tax incentives designed to encourage specific behavior, such as saving or donating to charity, often do not even reach those at lower income levels, thus providing no incentives to these citizens. If these incentives are to reach—and encourage particular behavior in—citizens of all income brackets, they must be made refundable. Refundable credits also would have the advantage of smoothing household income, softening the blow of economic hardships for those at lower income levels. In effect, this would smooth the macroeconomy, thus increasing economic efficiency.

Policymakers have created tax incentives for homeownership, retirement saving, education, and medical expenses. Other tax incentives seek to promote work, charitable giving, and investment in life insurance, annuities, and state and local bonds. Together, these tax incentives reduce federal tax revenues by about $500 billion a year, or roughly 4 percent of Gross Domestic Product. Structuring these tax incentives most efficiently is therefore an immensely important policy matter.

Approximately $420 billion of these existing tax incentives operate through deductions, exemptions, or exclusions. Such tax incentives tie the size of the tax break to an individual's marginal tax bracket: A deduction of $1, for example, is worth 35 cents to someone in the 35 percent marginal bracket but only 15 cents to someone in the 15 percent marginal bracket. Such incentives thus provide relatively weak incentives to those in low tax rate brackets. Furthermore, these types of tax incentives fail to reach the increasingly significant share of low- and moderate-income individuals and families who do not have any federal income tax liability to offset in any given year. More than 35 percent of households during any given year have no income tax liability; these households are home to almost half of all American children.

Refundable tax credits represent a different approach. Since they are a credit, rather than a deduction or exclusion, they do not depend on a household's marginal tax bracket. A tax credit of $1, for example, reduces taxes by $1 and thus is worth the same to households in the 35 percent bracket or the 15 percent bracket. And since they are refundable, they provide benefits to all tax filers, regardless of whether they owe income taxes on net.

The Growth of Refundable Tax Credits

Currently the tax code contains three main refundable tax credits: the Earned Income Tax Credit, the Child Tax Credit, and a small health insurance credit. The Earned Income Tax

Credit (EITC) is the largest anti-poverty program for the non-elderly in the country. In inflation-adjusted terms, the budgetary cost of the EITC has risen by a factor of nine since it was enacted in 1975, and it tripled between 1990 and 2000 alone. More recently, the partially refundable Child Tax Credit (CTC) [enacted in 1997] and the fully refundable health insurance credit [2002] were enacted, and the refundability of the CTC was expanded and accelerated.

Tax incentives are most efficient if they provide the same incentive to all households.

Several factors likely contributed to the dramatic growth of refundable credits over the past three decades. For example, policymakers have increasingly relied on the tax code rather than direct government expenditures to subsidize households and influence their behavior as a result of perceived or real incentives within the tax legislative process, a development that has supported the rise of refundable credits.

Despite the growth in refundable credits, most tax incentives intended to promote socially-beneficial behavior take the form of deductions or other approaches linked to marginal tax rates. Yet if policymakers want to broadly promote socially-valued behavior through the tax code, refundable credits are generally necessary. . . . In any given year more than one-third of households do not have any federal income tax liability. About a quarter of tax units file a tax return but have no income tax liability, and another 13 percent do not file. Moreover, almost half of all children, and 80 percent of children in single parent households, live in tax units with no income tax liability in any given year.

As a result, if policymakers want to create incentives through the individual income tax for all or most tax units to engage in certain behavior every year, such as saving or obtaining education for themselves or their children, refundability should not only be considered an acceptable instrument of tax policy—it is imperative.

Furthermore, unless there is evidence that certain households are more responsive to the incentive than others or generate larger social benefits from engaging in the activity, tax incentives are most efficient if they provide the same incentive to all households—and that can only be accomplished in a straightforward manner through a uniform (and refundable) credit.

The Benefits of Uniform Incentives

The reason that a uniform incentive is the most efficient approach in the absence of evidence regarding differences in responsiveness or social benefits is that a small number of large mistakes in under- or over-subsidizing an activity are more costly in efficiency terms than a large number of small mistakes. For example, imagine that certain behavior, perhaps charitable contributions, on average generates 5 cents of social benefits per dollar contributed per year and policymakers have determined to subsidize contributions by, on average, 5 cents per dollar. Imagine further that there is a 50 percent chance that a dollar of contributions by a high-income household generates 10 cents of social benefits, while a dollar of contributions by a low-income household generates none, and a 50 percent chance that this pattern is reversed. A uniform subsidy of 5 cents would leave 5 cents of lost social benefits in both cases. Meanwhile, a subsidy of 10 cents given to one group would result in 10 cents of lost social benefits in one case and none in the other. The uniform subsidy is more efficient—it technically minimizes the "expected deadweight loss"—because a small number of big errors (one case of 10 cents) is more costly than a large number of small errors (two cases of 5 cents).

We acknowledge that many behavioral tax incentives may be bad policy regardless of whether they take the form of uniform refundable credits, perhaps because the behavior in question does not actually generate social benefits or because such social benefits are best addressed through direct government provision of the good or regulation. Even taking these limitations into account, however, assuming the continued existence of a tax incentive, our default structure is generally preferable because it minimizes the expected social losses from the tax incentive, regardless of whether the behavior actually is socially beneficial.

Weigh the Evidence

We also acknowledge that tax incentives should not provide the same incentive to all households in all circumstances. If there is evidence that the associated social benefits vary systematically by income class, or that different income groups exhibit different levels of responsiveness to the subsidy, the tax incentive should not be identical for all households. Indeed these differences between various income groups surely exist in reality. But when, as is frequently the case, the evidence on these issues is non-existent or inconclusive, the most efficient form for a tax incentive is a uniform refundable credit. The burden of proof should therefore be on those who prefer some other form of tax incentive to demonstrate that such deviations from a uniform refundable credit are justified by empirical evidence.

Uniform refundable credits can help stabilize macroeconomic demand fluctuations by raising cash payments to families during recessionary periods.

Thus, if policymakers wish to use the tax system to create incentives for certain socially-valued behavior, it makes no sense to exclude more than a third of American individuals and families from their reach, or to provide smaller benefits to some households than others, absent evidence that those Americans would be relatively unresponsive or that their behavior generates fewer societal benefits. Moreover, even when there is empirical evidence suggesting that the optimal tax incentive should not be the same for all households, the most efficient incentive is almost certainly still some type of refundable credit. It is extremely unlikely that there is a sharp break in social benefits or responsiveness to an incentive exactly at the point of no income tax liability, and these types of discontinuities are inherent in the application of all other basic forms of tax incentives.

A Smoothing Effect

The potential benefits of refundable credits are magnified further by a second feature: their ability to help smooth household income. That is, during hard years, transforming existing tax incentives into uniform refundable credits would boost after-tax income, and thus help to cushion the blow of a drop in earnings, unemployment, or other hardships. Such income smoothing is desirable for several reasons. It can reduce the costs associated with economic instability and offset failures in insurance markets. It also allows families to plan their expenditures more confidently and avoids the additional costs (such as moving costs and credit card debt) of financing constant changes in household living standards. Income smoothing is particularly beneficial for lower-income households because they generally don't have easy access to credit to make it through tough times, because they tend to have more volatile incomes than other families in general, and because income shocks can result in declines in their economic circumstances that persist over long periods of time and are passed on to their children.

The final element of the case for uniform refundable credits is their ability to smooth the macroeconomy. Like household income smoothing, macroeconomic smoothing can enhance economic efficiency. In particular, macroeconomic demand fluctuations make it difficult for companies to optimize their investment and production functions, resulting in adjustment costs. These difficulties can inhibit domestic and foreign investment, which is correlated with economic growth. As a result, there is broad consensus in support of taxing and spending policies that are automatically countercyclical. Uniform refundable credits can help stabilize macroeconomic demand fluctuations by raising cash payments to families during recessionary periods, which then helps to boost spending—precisely the desired response during such periods.

A Practical Proposal

William Gale of Brookings [Institution], Jonathan Gruber of MIT [Massachusetts Institute of Technology], and Peter Orszag of Brookings have recently proposed a specific example that is similar in spirit to our broader policy suggestion. They note that current incentives for contributions to 401(k) [employer-sponsored retirement] plans and IRAs [Individual Retirement Accounts] deliver their largest immediate benefits to higher-income individuals in the highest tax brackets.

Concerns about the extent of governmental redistribution ... do not justify rejecting refundable credits that are enacted to enhance economic efficiency.

Gale, Gruber, and Orszag would replace the existing tax deductions for contributions to retirement saving accounts with a 30 percent government matching contribution. Unlike the current system, workers' contributions to employer-based 401(k) accounts would no longer be excluded from income subject to taxation, and contributions to IRAs would no longer be tax deductible. Furthermore, any employer contributions to a 401(k) plan would be treated as taxable income to the employee (just as current wages are). However, all qualified employer and employee contributions would be eligible for the 30 percent government matching contribution regardless of the employee's income. This proposal would be roughly revenue neutral for the federal government, according to estimates from the Tax Policy Center microsimulation model.

This proposal provides a specific example of how a tax deduction or exclusion could be transformed, on a revenue neutral basis, into a uniform refundable credit. Our analysis generally supports this transformation as the default structure for retirement savings incentives, assuming such incentives are intended to promote the social benefits generated by retirement savings and that no other aspects of the tax code are intended to play that role.

Uniform refundable tax credits are generally the most efficient structure for a tax incentive to encourage desired behavior.

Opposition to Refundable Credits

Opponents of refundable credits typically raise four main concerns. First, some question the extent to which government should engage in redistribution between different income groups. Second, some argue that the tax system should be used only to raise revenue, not to provide subsidies. Third, some believe that all Americans should pay at least some tax, even if just one dollar, as a duty of citizenship and so that they feel some stake in governmental decisions. Finally, some argue that refundable credits would increase administrative and compliance costs on net and are particularly subject to fraud and abuse.

Concerns about the extent of governmental redistribution, however, do not justify rejecting refundable credits that are enacted to enhance economic efficiency by subsidizing socially-beneficial behavior. And concerns about delivering subsidies through the tax system instead of the transfer system are generally objections to tax incentives overall, not to structuring tax incentives as refundable credits specifically.

The third objection—that Americans should pay some tax—ignores the fact that most households claiming refundable credits pay a variety of federal, state and local taxes other than income taxes. Moreover, if one is interested strictly in federal income taxes, it seems likely that most refundable credit beneficiaries pay a positive amount of federal income tax over time as a result of the income variations that people tend to experience over their lives. Indeed, a simplified model of 2003 federal income tax law using data from the Panel Survey of Income Dynamics suggests that about three-quarters of tax units who are eligible for the refundable element of the EITC or CTC at some point during a 20-year period would nevertheless have positive net federal income tax liability over that period if historic earnings patterns are any guide. Thus, even if one accepts the principle that paying some income tax is necessary for feeling a stake in government decisions (which we do not), this principle would not necessarily preclude refundable credits once income tax liabilities are examined over longer time periods.

Risks Are Offset by Benefits

The final objection to refundable credits is that they could increase fraud and related compliance problems. Yet there is no reason in theory, and no empirical evidence in practice, why there should be a "cliff effect" in fraud precisely at the point of positive income tax liability. If anything, fraud may be easier to hide when it comes in the form of a deduction or exclusion, which reduces taxable income, as opposed to a refundable credit. Instead, reducing fraud and related compliance problems for all tax incentives, including refundable credits, requires structuring the incentives simply, relying on third-party reporting, and investing in enforcement staffing.

We recognize that increasing the prevalence of refundable credits may create incentives for tax units who are currently non-filers to begin filing, thereby increasing administrative costs for the government and compliance costs for these households. These costs are real and should be taken into account. Nevertheless, they should not be overstated. Currently only about 13 percent of tax units are non-filers. As a result, non-filers represent a relatively small share of the households who stand to gain from structuring tax incentives as uniform refundable credits. Moreover, all tax incentives are elective and, even for non-filers, the administrative and compliance costs associated with claiming them are likely to be swamped in many instances by the dollar value of the credit.

Uniform refundable tax credits are generally the most efficient structure for a tax incentive to encourage desired behavior when, as frequently occurs, evidence of how the desired behavior and its associated social benefits vary across the income distribution is unavailable or inconclusive. Indeed refundable tax credits are generally the only way to ensure a tax incentive reaches the roughly two-fifths of tax units with no positive income tax liability in a given year. These efficiency benefits are magnified by the ability of refundable credits to help smooth income at a household level and by their ability, to a greater or less extent, to bolster the role of the tax system as an automatic stabilizer of macroeconomic demand. The United States spends almost 4 percent of GDP [gross domestic product] each year subsidizing socially-valued activities through the tax code. Our proposal would dramatically improve the effectiveness and fairness of this substantial investment.

8

Reducing Corporate Taxes Would Strengthen the Economy

Thomas G. Donlan

Thomas G. Donlan is the editorial page editor at Barron's. *He has written columns about the economy, politics, and investing for more than 15 years.*

The corporate income tax punishes successful companies and results in higher prices for consumers. It is the first step in a system of double taxation on capital that discourages investment. The corporate tax also adds to the complexity of the tax code, thereby raising Internal Revenue Service operating costs. In the global context, the U.S. has the second-highest corporate tax rate in the world, which hinders its ability to compete with other countries to attract new business. While U.S. politicians, in Congress and the Treasury, have voiced concern about the corporate tax, nothing has been done about it yet. House Ways and Means Committee Chairman Charles Rangel has proposed a modest rate reduction but he would pay for this reduction by increasing other business taxes. Congress should, at least, make the corporate income tax simpler. The best solution, however, would be to eliminate the tax entirely.

Our stubborn habit at each turning of the year is to denounce the injustice and impracticality of the corporate income tax. It is a tax on economic success and amounts to left-handed favoritism for unprofitable companies. It is an invisible tax on customers, who pay higher prices when the corporate income tax is passed down the line.

Paying taxes on profits—the fuel for the economic engine—is bad enough when it happens only once, but the corporate income tax is the first step in a two-step tax on capital. Corporate profits are taxed, then taxed again when distributed to the owners of the business as dividends and capital gains. The double-dipping doubly discourages investors and investment.

Then there are the indirect costs of the corporate income tax, which probably are worse than the direct burdens. It mandates complexity in the calculation of revenues and expenses, which in turn requires a corps of auditors and lawyers at the Internal Revenue Service [IRS], which in turn requires a bigger corps of accountants and tax counsels at every corporation. These people could have been employed in more productive endeavors. The Tax Foundation estimates that the total expense of compliance sucked $147 billion out of businesses in 2005. (The direct cost of business taxation was $278 billion.)

There is more to the corporate tax than just the domestic economic impact. Whether Americans know it or not, the United States and its businesses are in constant competition with businesses based in other countries. It should not be a surprise that costs of doing business vary around the world, and that taxes in most countries are a significant business cost.

Taxes on world trade are levied according to a set of rules that penalize the United States for its reliance on corporate income taxes.

The U.S. has so many other positive attributes for business—skilled workers, deep capital resources, relatively low regulation and open markets, for example—that it has thought itself able to afford to neglect its competitive position on taxes. The United States is far behind most of the world in the effort to provide attractive tax rates.

An Uncompetitive Rate

The U.S. rate of 35% (it's 40% if the average impact of state corporate income taxes is included) is the second-highest in the world, after Japan's.

Competition is getting stiffer. The average corporate tax bite in the 17 most-developed countries was 31% in 2006, down from 38% in 1994 and 51% in 1982, according to the Organization for Economic Cooperation and Development [OECD]. The last significant reduction in the U.S. federal corporate tax rate was the cut from 50% to 34% that came as part of the 1986 tax reform.

Even China, a nation of nominal communists, has a corporate tax rate of 25%. The leaders of Vietnam and France have announced their intentions to take their corporate rates to the same 25% level.

Some of the most dramatic cuts in corporate income tax since 1982 have been tallied in Germany (62% to 39%), Britain (52% to 30%), Sweden (61% to 28%) and Austria (62% to 27%). At 12%, Ireland has the lowest corporate income-tax rate of the 17 countries, and Ireland also has been the best economic performer in Western Europe.

Rates are not the whole story; each country defines its taxable-income base differently, and each country builds its own loopholes to favor certain industries. The U.S. ranks only fifth of the OECD 17 in terms of the average take from the corporate income tax. But it is rates more than takes that declare intentions, and it is clear to every capitalist in the world that the United States does not intend to allow businesses to keep all the fruits of their efforts.

Self-Punishing Policy

Taxes on world trade are levied according to a set of rules that penalize the United States for its reliance on corporate income taxes. Under the rules of the World Trade Organization, value-added taxes need not be levied if the taxed goods or services are exported. No such export rebate is allowed for corporate income taxes. If a German car might be liable for $5,000 of value-added tax, its manufacturer would receive the $5,000 back from the tax authorities after driving the car onto a ship bound for the United States. A Honda exported from these shores would carry its share of the manufacturer's corporate income tax across the ocean, with no rebate allowed.

The U.S. Congress goes on year after year holding hearings about this inequity, and the U.S. goes on and on running up trade deficits, but nothing is ever done to secure better tax treatment for our exports by substituting a value-added tax for the corporate income tax, or by negotiating equal treatment for both kinds of taxation.

The easiest and best way forward is to remove the corporate income tax entirely.

The abolition of the corporate income tax is our favorite cause, but even with our rose-colored glasses on we don't see very many hints of future success.

The last two secretaries of the U.S. Treasury have spoken out against the tax. Unfortunately, the power of that office is much overrated, so they haven't helped the cause as much as we might wish.

The holder of a much more powerful office, House Ways & Means Committee Chairman Charles Rangel, has offered a small slice off the tax, proposing [in 2007] to cut the rate from 35% to 30.5%. Any cut would be better than nothing, except that Rangel actually was offering something worse than nothing. All the lost tax revenue would be made up by increasing other taxes. The top rate on the ordinary income tax, which includes the tax on many small businesses, would rise from 35% to 44% in Rangel's plan.

Simplify or Eliminate

At the very least, Chairman Rangel and his cohorts in Congress should make the federal corporate income tax less complex and less burdensome. They could turn down the heat on capital by permitting immediate expensing of investments. That would also reduce the number of accountants and lobbyists needed to play games with investment-tax credits and depreciation and the number of IRS agents needed to referee the games.

Perhaps more important, considering the recent American experience with excessive debt, Congress should redress the tax imbalance that favors corporate borrowing over corporate equity. Such differentials only enrich the inventors of tax shelters. We could end the expensing of interest payments, but the easiest and best way forward is to remove the corporate income tax entirely.

9

Reducing Corporate Taxes Weakens the Economy

Kristian Weise

Kristian Weise is a policy research officer with the International Trade Union Confederation. He served on the steering committee for the World Bank's Researchers Alliance for Development in 2007.

Corporate tax rates have been falling worldwide for several years, at the same time that businesses are finding more loopholes to avoid paying taxes. Both of these trends could lead to a global economic crisis. It is commonly thought that smaller countries are the ones that most frequently cut taxes to attract new business, but in fact, some of the countries with the largest economies, such as the U.S. and Japan, have lost the most corporate tax revenue in the past few decades. Simultaneously, corporate profits have boomed while wages have halted. Thus, the burden of remaining competitive in the global market has fallen primarily on workers and consumers rather than corporations themselves. Continuing to cut corporate tax rates will result in a further loss of revenue for governments and a decline in economic activity. To avoid an economic crisis, corporations must pay more of their share of the overall tax burden.

"In this world nothing is certain but death and taxes", Benjamin Franklin once famously said. But for corporations, paying taxes is anything but a certainty. Statutory corporate

Kristian Weise, "Corporate Tax Warning," *The OECD Observer*, vol. 261, May 2007, pp. 22–23. Copyright © 2007 OECD Observer. Reproduced by permission. www. oecdobserver.org.

tax rates are plummeting in most countries, while business keeps finding ever more creative ways of getting around paying any taxes at all—leveraging debt in privately held corporations being the most recent trend of this. While the OECD [Organisation for Economic Co-operation and Development] has put itself in the driver's seat of the international effort to combat tax evasion and avoidance in the form of transfer pricing and the use of tax havens, the detrimental tax competition that many of its own member economies are engaging in has so far been receiving scant attention. Yet if more attention isn't given to this issue we could soon face a global tax crisis.

Within the last 20 years, corporate tax rates have fallen from around 45% to less than 30% on average in OECD countries. And lately, with increased mobility of multinational corporations, tax competition has intensified. Thus from 2000 to 2005, 24 out of the 30 OECD countries lowered their corporate tax rates while no member economy raised its rates. The consequence is that average rates in all OECD countries dropped from 33.6% in 2000 to 28.6% in 2005.

If tax on corporate dividends increasingly eludes national taxation, then taxing corporate profits should be the obvious place to find compensation.

The conventional wisdom is that it is primarily small economies that feel compelled to cut corporate taxes in order to attract foreign investments—Ireland and a handful of the newest EU [European Union] members are often put forward as examples of this—but it is actually some of largest economies in the world that have lost most tax revenue from corporations over the last decades. Most notably, between 1970 and 2003, corporate taxation as a share of total taxation dropped by 51% in Japan and by 39% in the US and in Germany. And from 1995 only, the weight of corporate taxation to public finances dropped by around 20% in the US, Japan and Italy.

The Shifting Tax Burden

Yet at the same time corporate profits are booming and wages are stagnating. After-tax profits in the US are, as a proportion of GDP [gross domestic product], at their highest in 75 years, and in the euro area and Japan they are also close to 25-year highs. Wages, on the other hand, are making up an ever smaller part of national income, down from 68% in 1982 to 59% in 2005 in the 15 EU members. And at 56.9% in the US in 2005, they are, except for a brief period in 1997, at their lowest level since 1966. Hence, relying on the income and spending of wage earners to fund ever larger parts of public finances will either hollow out government budgets or lower workers' incomes.

Other developments emphasise the mistiming of the present corporate tax break. Business increasingly bases its success on institutional and societal competitiveness—in short the qualities of the societies they are part of, such as the skills of their workforce, publicly funded research and infrastructure, and well-developed legal systems and intellectual property regimes. As a result, more and more government spending is used to enhance such competitiveness. Yet surely corporations, as beneficiaries of these investments, should pay their share in taxation. Surely the burden should not fall on workers or on consumption. For the sake of both equity and efficiency, business tax cannot be allowed to go on falling. And with ownership structures of private business becoming more international on a daily basis, corporate profits in the form of dividends increasingly escape national tax collection and thus contribute nothing to the spending and investments necessary to maintain and extend institutional and societal competitiveness. If tax on corporate dividends increasingly eludes national taxation, then taxing corporate profits should be the obvious place to find compensation.

Tax Cuts Must Be Limited

Corporate tax competition inevitably leads to declines in the amount of taxes paid by corporations, a loss of public revenue in many cases, particularly if economic activity is slack, and a greater burden on individuals. Since tax bases have been broadened while rates have been cut, globally the corporate tax crisis is still at bay. But there is a limit to how much corporate tax bases can be broadened. And in the OECD countries in particular, this limit is not far away. Even the broadest tax base will not matter if tax rates tend towards zero. And this might happen earlier than we think. If the linear trends in the OECD countries are extrapolated into the future, statutory corporate tax rates will hit zero by the middle of this century.

Is there any choice but to step up initiatives on harmful tax practices and discourage unfair tax rivalry?

The somewhat tragic irony is that the countries that have participated most actively in this downward tax competition haven't even had the short-term gains in the form of increased foreign direct investment that motivated them to do so. The reason is simple: cutting tax to attract investment cannot work on its own and may be counterproductive. Take Ireland, often held up as a low tax success story. Yet Ireland's inward investment and robust economic growth owe much to a strong public sector and smart use of tax spending in areas like education and infrastructure, not just to its tax cuts. It would be foolhardy to think that any country can emulate Ireland's success by cutting taxes. In fact, given the need to build up their frameworks, they may end up damaging their prospects. Little wonder that research shows that the "new" member states of the European Union haven't received more investments from the "old" member states in the years they have aggressively cut their corporate tax rates. Elsewhere, in G7 [Group of Seven industrialized nations of the world] Canada, a cut in the statutory corporate tax rate from 28% to 21% between 2000 and 2006 was followed by a decline in net inflows of FDI [foreign direct investment] in the same period.

An Impending Tax Crisis

Without action, we could be on the verge of a global tax crisis that could hurt economic activity. The tax burden cannot be carried by labour and consumption alone. The upshot of inaction would be a loss of revenue for governments and a downward spiral in economic activity. Governments must realise that "beggar-thy-neighbour" tax competition risks eroding their own economic and social foundations. And they must recognise that all countries have a common interest in cooperating to achieve fair levels of corporate taxation. This requires multilateral solutions.

The message that tax systems enable growth and that corporations must pay their share surely makes sense to most governments. Is there any choice but to step up initiatives on harmful tax practices and discourage unfair tax rivalry? The EU has taken a first step by starting work on creating a common corporate tax base. Yet while positive in itself much further initiatives must be taken, both within and outside the EU, to address the fragility of current corporate tax practices. Political will and dedication is needed, but the public gains would be worth it. Surely that is what co-operation and development [are] all about.

10

Repealing the Estate Tax Would Benefit the Economy

Don Rogers

Don Rogers served for 18 years in the California state legislature, where he led the successful campaign to abolish the inheritance and gift taxes in that state.

Stories of family business owners selling their businesses before they die, to spare their heirs the burden of the estate tax, are commonplace. Unfortunately, such sales mean a loss of livelihood for remaining family members, as well as a loss of jobs for the surrounding communities, because the buyers are often large companies. Under current U.S. law, the estate tax will decline until total repeal in 2010. But in 2011, it will reappear at an even higher rate of 55 percent. Permanently repealing this tax would avoid many unpleasant situations for business-owning families. Advocates of the estate tax argue that it ensures that inheritance is not spent selfishly and, instead, is used for the common good. In fact, the estate tax actually hurts the economy by discouraging investment and prompting noncompliance with tax laws. Possibly the most inefficient tax, the estate tax also costs the government a lot of money to enforce and oversee. Even if eliminating the estate tax reduced federal revenues, the U.S. population is still more than large enough to fund necessary government programs. Rather than reducing the estate tax or increasing exemptions, the estate tax should be eradicated.

The Milner family started their farm-equipment business in Kern County, California, in 1950, and after 30 years it had grown to 20 locations and employed 300 employees. Mr. Milner was an excellent businessman who had developed a very successful operation through careful planning. Being aware that upon his death his estate would be hit with a 55-percent death tax on the full value of his assets, he realized the best course of action for his heirs would be to sell out early and pay a 20-percent capital-gains tax instead of the 55-percent federal death tax. However, his decision also meant that his family would no longer have a family business, and his children would not have an opportunity to work in the family business. The buyer was a large foreign public company that, shortly after purchase, radically changed the operation. The jobs of most of the 20-year veteran employees were terminated by the new foreign owners.

According to the Policy and Taxation Group, which monitors such activities, this is not an unusual story. Many family businesses sell out early to reduce the horrendous burden of the estate tax. This means that families lose their businesses and livelihoods, and jobs are lost in the community. Much of the job loss is a result of who buys the businesses: large public companies and foreign business interests, which are not subject to the estate tax, buy up the small- and medium-sized family businesses.

Under current law, the "Federal Estate Tax" (death tax) will decline over time and be totally repealed in 2010—heirs will pay zero dollars in federal inheritance tax—but then in 2011, the tax will be reimposed at a top rate of 55 percent and an exemption of $1 million. If you are in poor health in 2010 and own substantial business or personal assets, your heirs might pray for your prompt departure into the hereafter. Hopefully, they won't "prey" on you and ensure your departure.

A Devastating Tax

In 2011, if an owner of a small business, farm, or ranch with assets of $2 million were to pass away, the heirs of the estate would have to pay federal estate taxes of about $550,000! This tax doesn't only apply to children who inherit: when one spouse dies, the survivor must pay out for "inherited assets." Oftentimes the heirs of such property inherit very little cash with the property, so the heirs are forced to sell the business or part of the farm or ranch to raise enough cash to pay the tax collector, who may be knocking on the door before the funeral is over.

All of the assets, whether cash, equipment, or land, have already been fully taxed when the assets were acquired.

A permanent repeal of the federal estate tax would avoid many tax-planning headaches and unpleasant family situations. In South Dakota, the owner of a farm, in an attempt to lessen the devastation of the federal death tax, began gifting several acres of the farm to his son each year. After many years almost all of the farm was vested in the son. Then the son was tragically killed in an accident. Since the father then inherited the farm, the father had to sell almost all of the land to pay the federal death tax. He was only able to keep the home and the barn. Then he had to lease the acreage from the new owner in order to continue working the farm.

Jennylynne and her family live in Lone Jack, Missouri. Jennylynne's parents had been in the electrical construction business for over 20 years, and Jennylynne learned the business working with her parents. When her parents started talking about retirement and turning the business over to Jennylynne, the parents became aware of the estate tax and gift tax that would have to be paid at their death. The family considered borrowing against the assets to pay the tax, but the business could not support the debt at the interest rates that would have to be paid. After 20 years in the business, the company's assets were sold to outsiders, who then terminated many of the employees. Sadly, the sale of the assets so devastated Jennylynne's father that he died 14 months later. Her father could not understand why he could not pass his business to his daughter who had worked by his side for years.

A Second Dose of Taxes

Remember, all of the assets, whether cash, equipment, or land, have already been fully taxed when the assets were acquired. They were subject to the income tax, payroll tax, sales tax, and capital-gains tax. Then, just because there is a death in the family, all of those inherited assets are heavily taxed again. It appears to be closer to confiscation than merely taxation, doesn't it?

People of a socialist bent criticize families who try to maintain their assets and then pass them on to their heirs, saying they are selfish and their money would be better used serving the public good. The big-government crowd has even introduced a phrase called "The Tax Expenditure," based on their fallacy that all money and wealth belongs to government, and that any reduction in revenue to any level of government would therefore be a "tax expenditure." Coincidentally, the "abolition of all rights of inheritance" is the third of 10 planks of the *Communist Manifesto*, which was written by Karl Marx and Friedrich Engels to explain how to transform an industrialized country into a socialist/communist country. Yet it is the preservation and accumulation of capital that fuels economic growth and creates more real jobs.

The estate tax hurts the economy by suppressing investment and causing unproductive tax-avoidance activity. According to an article by the Tax History Project entitled "A Century of Soaking the Rich," this negative impact was foreseen. When passage of the estate tax was being debated before its inception in 1916, Rep. Edward Cooper (R) "insisted that all efforts to soak the rich and spare the poor were doomed to failure. 'No taxation, whether direct or indirect, can in the end be levied which will not be a burden on the whole people.'" Hindsight shows that Cooper was a very smart man. Because of the estate tax, the poor find fewer job opportunities (their "burden" from the tax). The reason behind this truth is because people naturally try to avoid being taxed, or if they can't avoid it, they plan for it.

Discouraging Investment

In trying to escape taxes, research done by the CONSAD Research Corporation in 2003 shows that at about age 75, people begin to lock in the assets that they have accrued. Productive owners decide to slow down, reduce their investment, and increase their consumption as they age. Tax law professor Edward McCaffery says "the death tax discourages savings and rewards a selfish 'die-broke' ethic." Owners stop reinvesting their money because they understand that most of what they make will go to the government anyway. By doing so, they deprive the economy of seed money to begin or expand businesses. (They also deprive the government of money in the way of additional capital-gains taxes.)

A study done by Carnegie Mellon University ... concluded that repealing the death tax would generate more revenues for government.

Alternately, when businesses try to plan for the death tax, "Resources are diverted from the operation of their business to procure estate-planning services and to set aside reserves or purchase life insurance in anticipation of the eventual payment of the estate tax. If the estate tax were eliminated, these resources would become available for business purposes," said CONSAD. Karen Oman of Minneapolis told the Policy and Taxation Group about her family's experience in this area:

"We just recently learned that we would not have the cash to pay estate taxes if we were to die. The company would be liquidated. Life insurance would cost up to $45,000 per year for $2,000,000 in coverage, which would still not cover all estate taxes. We're in limbo on what to do."

Repealing Tax Would Increase Revenue

CONSAD's computer modeling demonstrated that if the estate tax were repealed in 2003 and a very slight modification of capital-gains taxes were implemented, there would be "a cumulative net increase in government tax revenues equal to $38.0 billion over the period from 2003 to 2012. That net increase will consist of $231.2 billion in additional revenues from the capital-gains tax and personal income tax, which will more than offset the foregone $193.0 billion in estate-tax revenues." A study done by Carnegie Mellon University in Pittsburgh last year [2006] also concluded that repealing the death tax would generate more revenues for government.

In fact, the net increase to the government would likely be much greater than $38 billion because the estate tax is probably the most inefficient tax of all. It is very difficult for the government to administer and enforce. There is an overflow of high-paid lawyers and accountants doing litigation, asset appraisals, and paperwork. And as Alicia Munnell, a member of President Bill Clinton's Council of Economic Advisers, estimated: "The resources spent on avoiding estate taxes may be as large as the amount that the tax collects."

The best solution to the "death tax" abomination is to permanently bury it.

To support the concept that average workers would gain from repeal of the estate tax, Greg Mankiw, former chairman of President George W. Bush's Council of Economic Advisers, noted that as a tax on capital, the estate tax reduces U.S. productivity and wages. He concluded that "repeal of the estate tax would stimulate growth and raise incomes for everyone." Also, President George W. Bush has been very consistent in asking for the complete repeal of the federal estate tax as an important part of his proposed tax reduction package.

Starved into Submission

Many countries, including India, New Zealand, Sweden, Switzerland, and Thailand, have decided that they do not want an estate tax, and these countries have benefited by not placing this burden on their economies. The two countries with the highest "death tax" rate are Japan (70 percent) and the United States (still 45 percent, it's being phased out, reaching zero in 2010 before shooting back up to its previous high of 55 percent in 2011). Japan, the world's second-biggest economy, has been mired in a slow-motion deflation since the early 1990s. Whole sections of Japan's construction and financial sectors continue to stagnate. Their high "death tax" rate is not the only reason for this stagnation, but is certainly a strong contributing factor.

But even if getting rid of the death tax were to result in an overall reduction in federal revenues, that would be a good thing! With our expanding population, under the present taxing system, the United States collects more than enough money to fund all of our constitutionally authorized government programs, including a strong military.

As a senator in the state of California, I was convinced that the only way to slow the growth and power of government on every level is to give them less money at every opportunity. This means not supporting any proposed tax increase, fee increase, assessment increase, or any bonds, and only electing candidates who share this belief. The only way to keep government under any semblance of control is to starve it into submission. This is not only good for businesses competing in a global economy; it's in the best interests of individuals, no matter what their income level.

The best solution to the "death tax" abomination is to permanently bury it. Any compromise, such as reducing the percentage rate or increasing the exemption level, will leave the door open for future spendthrift Congresses and administrations to merely reinstate higher and higher rates and lower exemption levels. Just get rid of it.

11

Modifying the Estate Tax into an Inheritance Tax Would Benefit the Economy

The Economist

The Economist is a weekly newspaper based in London that supports free trade and globalization. Authors are not named in order to emphasize the content over the creators.

Estate taxes have historically affected a very small amount of the British and American populations, but many nonwealthy people have begun to worry that they will face such taxes. While the estate tax may be politically unpopular, it is, for the most part, economically sound. It preserves an incentive for heirs to continue working, prevents the rise of a plutocracy, and is implicitly fair. However, the estate tax could be far simpler and, thus, would be more effective if it were transformed into a true inheritance tax. This tax would actually prevent wealth inequality even better than the estate tax does. It would also allow different tax rates to be set according to the closeness of heirs to the donor.

Taxes on estates when their owners die arouse passions that politicians ignore at their peril. In America there has been a long-standing campaign to get rid of the federal "death tax". Thanks to George [W.] Bush's tax cuts, it is supposed to be repealed in 2010, though only for one year. In Britain a recent proposal by the opposition Conservatives to slash the burden of inheritance tax swung the polls their way to such an extent that Gordon Brown, the Labour prime minister, cancelled an election he had planned . . . autumn [2007].

The current unpopularity of death duties is perplexing considering how long they have been around. America introduced its federal estate tax in 1916. Britain's death duty goes back further. Taking modern shape in 1894, it can be traced back to 1694 when probate duty was introduced. Since 1986 it has confusingly been called inheritance tax although it is nothing of the sort. Like America's estate duty it remains a levy on the amount left by the deceased and does not tax what individual beneficiaries receive.

The hue and cry about death duties is all the more puzzling since they affect few people. In Britain, 6% of estates pay the levy, which raised less than 1% of total revenues in the . . . [2006] fiscal year. In America, between 1% and 2% of estates have typically been subject to the tax over the past two decades and it has contributed only about 1% of federal revenues.

The gut dislike of death duties seems to arise because the tax clashes with heartfelt dynastic instincts. Until recently this was a worry only for the super-rich, but now many ordinary people fear that, thanks to rising house prices, they may be dragged into paying death duties. Given the low take from the tax, it is easy to see why politicians on either side of the Atlantic have been so receptive to public worries. Cutting estate or inheritance tax seems to offer a big electoral hit at small fiscal cost.

The estate tax offers a modest counterweight against the development of a new plutocracy.

But good politics does not mean good economics. Taxes should be assessed on three grounds: how they affect incentives, how fair they are and how simple. Estate taxes score well on the first two, less satisfactorily on the third. Whatever their merits, however, a tax that targets beneficiaries, rather than the estate of the donor, would be more effective.

Better than Alternatives

Any tax on capital will tend to dissuade people from accumulating the wealth in the first place, but a death duty is arguably one of the better options. As Alan Auerbach, an economist at the University of California, Berkeley, pointed out in a lecture given in London ... [in 2006], it falls on unintended legacies—money put aside to pay for old age, for example—as well as intentional bequests. Since unintended bequests are, by definition, not planned they should be unaffected by the prospect of the tax.

Another argument for death duties is that big bequests make people less likely to work and to be enterprising. Winston Churchill put the argument succinctly in 1924 when he argued that the tax was "a certain corrective against the development of a race of idle rich". Economic research published at Syracuse University in America suggests that the more wealth that older people inherit, the more likely they are to quit the labour market.

Taxes on beneficiaries may have more political staying-power than old-style death duties.

The fiscal cost of abolishing death duties may seem trifling, but it still means that for a given level of public spending other taxes must rise, which may harm incentives more. This was a point readily appreciated by both Churchill in his 1925 budget and William Harcourt, who introduced estate duty in 1894. Both chancellors of the exchequer used extra revenues from death duties to lower the income tax.

Death duties can also be justified in terms of fairness. A thriving economy will generate great fortunes, but there is good reason to check these becoming entrenched through inheritance. The estate tax offers a modest counterweight against the development of a new plutocracy to rival the industrial barons of America's Gilded Age. Furthermore it also taxes wealth built up through windfalls rather than thrift and effort. For example, recent gains in the housing market have accrued mainly to people who happen to belong to the right generation and who own property in the right places.

Death by a Thousand Cuts

The case for retaining estate taxes in Britain and America is weaker on grounds of simplicity. In principle, the tax is quite straightforward; in practice it is anything but. It may not raise much revenue but it has been a goldmine for the tax-advice industry. In Britain the tax has generally fallen on the not-so-wealthy and the ill-advised.

The complexity of death duties is not a reason to do away with them but rather to reform them. By sticking with a tax on donors' estates, Britain and America have become the exception. Other developed countries now tax wealth received by beneficiaries. One advantage of this approach is that it does more to tackle wealth inequality, which arises from large inheritances rather than big estates. It creates an incentive for wealth to be spread among several beneficiaries, whereas the estate duty simply reduces the wealth that it taxes in a direct transfer to the state.

Another advantage of a genuine inheritance tax (not a false friend like Britain's) is that the tax authorities can set different rates according to how close heirs are to the donor. In France, for example, distant relatives are taxed more than children. Because this seems fairer for families, taxes on beneficiaries may have more political staying-power than old-style death duties.

Days after Mr. Brown's embarrassing retreat from an election, his chancellor announced measures that will enable more married couples and civil partners to pay lower death duties.

As so often, however, hasty decisions are not the best ones. The right way to take the sting out of the "death tax" is not to tinker with it through piecemeal cuts. Rather, the solution is to turn it into a levy on inheritance.

12

Reducing Taxes on Savings Would Benefit the Economy

Martin Feldstein

Martin Feldstein is the George F. Baker Professor of Economics at Harvard University. He served as President Ronald Reagan's chief economic adviser from 1982 to 1984.

The maximum tax rate for dividends and capital gains has been set at 15% since 2003. The President's Advisory Panel on Tax Reform wants this rate to be made permanent and extend to interest income. Congress should act on this proposal; otherwise, the rate will increase to 35% in 2008 and continue to rise. Income on savings should be taxed at a low rate or, even better, not at all. Taxing savings causes a distortion in the timing of consumption, worsening the negative effects of the income tax. It penalizes extra work, both saving and investing money. It is also a form of double taxation, because income is already taxed when it is first earned. Congress must prioritize reducing or eliminating the tax rates on savings.

Thanks to the tax legislation enacted in 2003, dividends and capital gains are now taxed at a maximum rate of 15%. The President's Advisory Panel on Tax Reform recently proposed [in 2005] that the 15% rate be made permanent and extended to interest income as well. If Congress does not act, the 2003 rule will expire and the rate will rise to 35% in 2008 and even higher in 2010.

Martin Feldstein, "Raise Taxes on Savings? Tell Joe It Ain't So!" *Wall Street Journal*, December 8, 2005, p. A16. Copyright © 2005 Dow Jones & Company, Inc. All rights reserved. Reprinted with permission of the author.

Keeping the low rates on the income from savings should now be the highest priority of tax reform. Eliminating the tax on such income would be even better.

Here's why. A tax on interest, dividends and capital gains creates a major distortion in the timing of consumption, and also exacerbates the adverse effects of the income tax on all aspects of work effort and personal productivity. Such distortions create unnecessary economic waste that lowers our standard of living. The combination of a lower tax rate on the income from savings and a revenue-neutral rise in the tax on earnings can produce a higher net reward for additional work and productivity, as well as a reduction in the distortion between consuming now and in the future. That would reduce the economic damage caused by the tax system while collecting the same total revenue with the same distribution of the tax burden.

Joe's future consumption would be substantially reduced by the higher tax.

An example will illustrate the harmful effect of high taxes on the income from savings and show how the tax reform could make taxpayers unambiguously better off. Think about someone—call him Joe—who earns an additional $1,000. If Joe's marginal tax rate is 35%, he gets to keep $650. Joe saves $100 of this for his retirement and spends the rest. If Joe invests these savings in corporate bonds, he receives a return of 6% before tax and 3.9% after tax. With inflation of 2%, the 3.9% after-tax return is reduced to a real after-tax return of only 1.9%. If Joe is now 40 years old, this 1.9% real rate of return implies that the $100 of savings will be worth $193 in today's prices when Joe is 75. So Joe's reward for the extra work is $550 of extra consumption now and $193 of extra consumption at age 75.

The Influence of Taxes on Future Savings

But if the tax rate on the income from saving is reduced to 15% as the tax panel recommends, the 6% interest rate would yield 5.1% after tax and 3.1% after both tax and inflation. And with a 3.1% real return, Joe's $100 of extra saving would grow to $291 in today's prices instead of just $193.

There are two lessons in this example, each of which identifies a tax distortion that wastes potential output and therefore unnecessarily lowers levels of real well-being. The first is that a tax on interest income is effectively also a tax on the reward for extra work, cutting the additional consumption at age 75 from $291 to just $193. Because the high tax rate on interest income reduces the reward for work (as well as the reward for saving), Joe makes choices that lower his pretax earnings—fewer hours of work, less work effort, less investment in skills, etc.

The second lesson that follows from the example is that the tax on interest income substantially distorts the level of future consumption even if Joe does not make any change in the amount that he saves. With the same $100 of additional saving, the higher tax rate reduces his additional retirement consumption from $291 to $193, a one-third reduction. If Joe responds to the lower real rate of return that results from the higher tax rate on interest by saving less, the distortion of consumption is even greater. For example, if Joe would save $150 out of the extra $1,000 of earnings when his real net return is 3.1% (instead of saving $100 when the real net return is 1.9%), his extra consumption at age 75 would be $436, more than twice as much as with the 35% tax rate. But the key point is that Joe's future consumption would be substantially reduced by the higher tax rate even if he does not change his savings.

Mutually Beneficial Taxation

Taken together, these two lessons imply that a lower tax rate on interest income, combined with a small increase in the tax on other earnings, could make Joe unambiguously better off while also increasing government revenue. More specifically, if reducing the tax on interest income from 35% to 15% had no effect on Joe's earnings or on his initial consumption spending, the government could collect the same present value of tax revenue from Joe by raising the tax on his $1,000 of extra earnings from $350 to $385. Although this would cut Joe's saving from $100 to $65 (if he keeps his initial consumption spending unchanged), the higher net return on that saving would give Joe the same consumption at age 75. In this way, Joe would be neither better off nor worse off.

But experience shows that Joe would alter his behavior in response to the lower tax rate. He would earn more at age 40 and would save more for retirement. This change of behavior makes Joe better off (or he wouldn't do it) and the extra earnings and interest income would raise government revenue above what it would be with a 35% tax rate. So Joe would be unambiguously better off with the lower tax rate on interest income and the government would collect more tax revenue.

Any tax on capital gains is unjustified because it is a combination of three separate unfair taxes.

A tax on the income from saving is not only wasteful but also a very unfair form of double taxation. Income is taxed when it is earned and then taxed again if the individual decides to postpone consumption. When Joe earns an extra $1,000 and saves $100 of it, he pays $350 in tax immediately and then an additional $157 in tax on his extra interest income until he reaches age 75. Why should Joe pay more tax on his $1,000 of earnings than a spendthrift who consumes all of his extra income at age 40?

Policy Should Encourage Investment

Although the example assumed Joe invested his savings in bonds, the case is even stronger for investment in stocks. The higher historic yield on stocks than on bonds reflects a reward for greater risk-taking. Taxing that higher pretax yield on stocks implies a greater loss of return and therefore a greater economic waste than the tax on bond interest. Taxing that reward for risk-taking also drives individuals away from stocks and into bonds and bank deposits, thereby depriving the economy of the equity investments needed for new ventures and business expansion.

Any tax on capital gains is unjustified because it is a combination of three separate unfair taxes. One part of the capital gains tax is a tax on the rise of a company's value that reflects the retained earnings that have already been subject to a corporate income tax and should not be taxed again. A second part of the capital gains tax reflects the rise in the nominal value of the company due to the rise in the general price level since the stock was purchased, a rise in nominal value that does not make the shareholder better off in real terms. The remaining part of the capital gains reflects the unpredictable variation in share prices that averages out to zero in an efficient capital market. If the tax law allowed full loss offsets when share prices fell, the government would collect no revenue from these variations; any net revenue reflects only the unfair limits on loss offsets.

Whatever else the [George W. Bush] administration and Congress do as part of the current tax reforms, cutting the tax on the return to savings should be at the top of the list.

13

Repealing the Alternative Minimum Tax Would Benefit the Economy

Mike Crapo

Mike Crapo is a Republican senator from Idaho, currently serving his second term. He is a member of several Senate committees, including the Budget and Finance committees.

The Alternative Minimum Tax (AMT) is an additional tax owed by those whose income tax is deemed too low for their income. It was originally set up to make sure that individuals at the highest income levels were not avoiding paying income taxes entirely. However, it is no longer serving its original purpose. Instead, it penalizes taxpayers who are married, have children or property, and disproportionately taxes farmers and ranchers. Furthermore, if the AMT is not reduced or repealed, it will affect taxpayers at moderate income levels as well because it was never indexed for inflation. By 2015, the AMT will affect almost half of all income tax filers. The AMT must be repealed before this happens, and before the federal government becomes even more dependent on its revenue.

> Still one thing more, fellow citizens—a wise and frugal government, which shall restrain men from injuring one another, which shall leave them otherwise free to regulate their own pursuits of industry and improvement, and shall

not take from the mouth of labor the bread it has earned. This is the sum of good government, and this is necessary to close the circle of our felicities.

—Thomas Jefferson (1743–1826), Third President of the United States, First Inaugural Address, March 4, 1801

I wonder if Thomas Jefferson would consider the collection of $95 billion dollars from American taxpayers in 2010 in the form of a 26 percent regressive tax wise *or* frugal? If the Alternative Minimum Tax (AMT) is left as is, this will be the result—a far cry from frugal, even farther from wise, and it will give 34 percent of Americans far less ability to, in Jefferson's words, "regulate their own pursuits of industry and improvement." As another tax season comes to a close, it's a good time to consider the wisdom in these words of a Founding Father and former President.

I can think of a number of things more interesting to read about than tax law, but few things affect our lives more. As tedious or complicated as it may seem, our country stands at a significant tax reform crossroad, and people need to be aware of the decisions that face our nation with regard to certain aspects of the federal income tax.

The Alternative Minimum Tax Is Outdated

One of the lesser-known aspects of the tax code has been gaining national attention and for good reason. The AMT is the tax paid when the government determines, through a complicated formula, that you haven't paid enough federal income tax in relation to your income. Created in 1969, the AMT was formulated to ensure that extremely high income individuals who, through the legal use of all deductions and exemptions available to them, were able to avoid owing any income tax at all. Initially, the AMT accomplished what it was designed to do but now, more than 35 years later, it's failing in its original intent.

At a Senate Finance Committee hearing . . . [in 2005], witnesses from the United States Treasury, the Congressional Budget Office and taxpayer advocacy groups testified to something some unsuspecting middle income taxpayers have recently discovered—the AMT unfairly burdens taxpayers and penalizes people who are married, have children and own property. This serious problem must be addressed immediately. With my colleagues on the Finance Committee, I have co-sponsored legislation that would repeal the individual AMT. If the AMT is left alone, middle income taxpayers will foot the bill for an increasing percentage of federal expenditures, making this unfair tax all the more difficult to repeal.

Farmers and ranchers are disproportionately affected by the AMT because many exclusions, credits and deductions they claim are disallowed.

The Truth About the AMT

Some facts about the AMT and its effects over the next five years demonstrate the urgency of this problem.

- AMT was never indexed for inflation. The minimum exemption amount in 1969 was $30,000. In today's dollars, that's approximately $157,000. The current exemption amount, when a temporary (but minor) increase runs out at the end of this year, is $45,000 for married couples and $33,750 for most single taxpayers. At this rate, 34 percent of individual filers will pay the AMT in 2010. Of these 30 million or so filers, 53 percent will have incomes of less than $100,000.

- AMT does not allow for personal (child) exemptions, deductions of state and local income taxes, and places many taxpayers in a higher marginal tax bracket.

- By 2010, AMT will exceed revenue from regular income tax by $95 billion, up from $14 billion in 2004. This means that like it or not, we will, by default and without a national debate about merits or deficiencies, have what amounts to a 26 percent regressive national tax supporting the majority of federal spending.

- It's estimated that the average AMT taxpayer owed an additional $6,000 in tax in 2004.

- The AMT requires millions of filers to compute their taxes *twice*, once to determine their standard tax liability and a second time (complete with a two-page form with eight pages of instructions) to determine if they are liable for the AMT.

- Farmers and ranchers are disproportionately affected by the AMT because many exclusions, credits and deductions they claim are disallowed under the AMT.

- The AMT was targeted to 155 wealthy potential taxpayers in 1969 who had legally avoided paying any income tax. In today's dollars, that would be the same thing as people making $1.1 million avoiding up to $400,000 in tax liability.

- A single parent with three children making less than $100,000 was eligible to file a 1040EZ [income tax form] because he had no itemized deductions. The fact that he claimed his children as dependents required him to pay the AMT.

- A married couple with four children and one in college both worked outside the home. They were required to pay AMT equal to their entire interest and dividend income for that year, in effect, invoking a 100 percent penalty for wisely investing their hard-earned money.

- The AMT contributes to the phenomenon of people making investment and expenditure choices that minimize their tax liability. This deals the economy a negative blow by discouraging savings and investments.

- Compliance costs increase in direct proportion to the increase in the reach of the AMT across a wider span of income levels.

We Must Repeal It Now

The cost of addressing the problem now is substantial, but still significantly less than if we wait even a few years down the road. In 2015, AMT will affect almost half of all individual filers, most unfairly, and the cost of repealing it at that point will eclipse the cost of repealing the regular income tax. This problem must be dealt with responsibly by looking at the potential for crisis in the near future. Immediate repeal, before we become further dependent upon revenues gained through AMT, is the wisest course of action.

Organizations to Contact

The editors have compiled the following list of organizations concerned with the issues debated in this book. The descriptions are derived from materials provided by the organizations. All have publications or information available for interested readers. The list was compiled on the date of publication of the present volume; the information provided here may change. Be aware that many organizations take several weeks or longer to respond to inquiries, so allow as much time as possible.

American Enterprise Institute for Public Policy Research
1150 Seventeenth Street NW, Washington, DC   20036
(202) 862-5800 • fax: (202) 862-7177
Web site: www.aei.org

The American Enterprise Institute for Public Policy Research is a private, nonpartisan research and education institution dedicated to defending the principles of democratic capitalism, such as limited government, individual liberty, and vigilant and effective defense and foreign policies. The organization sponsors research in three primary areas: economic policy, social and political studies, and defense and foreign policy. Publications include a monthly newsletter, *The American* magazine, Tax Policy Outlook essays, and numerous others.

The Brookings Institution
1775 Massachusetts Avenue NW, Washington, DC   20036
(202) 797-6000
Web site: www.brookings.edu

The Brookings Institution is a public-policy organization that emphasizes strengthening American democracy; supporting the economic and social welfare, security, and opportunity of all Americans; and securing a more open, safe, prosperous, and cooperative international system. It conducts independent research and provides recommendations based on this research. The organization publishes various newsletters, including the *Economic Studies Bulletin*, journals such as *Brookings Papers on Economic Activity*, and books such as *Using Taxes to Reform Health Insurance*.

Cato Institute
1000 Massachusetts Avenue NW, Washington, DC   20001
(202) 842-0200 • fax: (202) 842-3490
Web site: www.cato.org

The Cato Institute is a research foundation that promotes the principles of limited government, individual liberty, free markets, and peace. In addition to research, it provides educational information and encourages greater involvement of citizens in public-policy discussions. The institute's publications include the *Cato Journal*, *Cato Policy Report*, *Tax & Budget Bulletin*, and several others.

Center for American Progress
1333 H Street NW, 10th Floor, Washington, DC   20005
(202) 682-1611 • fax: (202) 682-1867
e-mail: progress@americanprogress.org
Web site: www.americanprogress.org

The Center for American Progress is a progressive think tank inspired by the social movements of the twentieth century, including civil rights, women's suffrage, and the labor movement. It is dedicated to improving the lives of Americans and focuses on such issues as climate change, universal health care, and economic opportunity for all. The center publishes issue alerts, reports such as *Progressive Growth: Transforming America's Economy*, and the newsletter *InProgress*.

Center on Budget and Policy Priorities
820 First Street NE, Suite 510, Washington, DC   20002
(202) 408-1080 • fax: (202) 408-1056
e-mail: center@cbpp.org
Web site: www.cbpp.org

The Center on Budget and Policy Priorities is an organization concerned with the effects of budget and tax policy on low-income families and individuals. It conducts research and analysis to inform public debates about economic policy and develops policy options to eliminate poverty. The Center publishes *Policy Points*, as well as other reports, analyses, and policy statements.

Citizens for Tax Justice

1616 P Street NW, Suite 200, Washington, DC   20036
(202) 299-1066 • fax: (202) 299-1065
Web site: www.ctj.org

Citizens for Tax Justice is a research and advocacy organization that seeks to give all citizens a voice in the debates about tax policy. It promotes tax policy that is fair for low- and middle-income Americans, that requires wealthy Americans to pay their fair share, that closes corporate loopholes, that funds important government services, that reduces the federal debt, and that minimizes the distortion of economic markets. The organization's publications include *The Tax Justice Digest* and policy statements such as *A Progressive Solution to the AMT Problem*.

The Club for Growth

2001 L Street, Suite 600, Washington, DC   20036
(202) 955-5500 • fax: (202) 955-9466
Web site: www.clubforgrowth.org

The Club for Growth is a network of citizens promoting economic freedom and growth. Its policy goals include death-tax repeal, cutting government spending, Social Security reform, free trade expansion, and regulatory reform. The Club for Growth publishes an annual Congressional Scorecard and House and Senate Repork Cards.

Economic Policy Institute

1333 H Street NW, Suite 300, East Tower
Washington, DC   20005

(202) 775-8810 • fax: (202) 775-0819
e-mail: epi@epi.org
Web site: www.epi.org

The Economic Policy Institute is a nonpartisan think tank that seeks to broaden economic policy debates to include the interests of low- and middle-income workers. It conducts research and informs and empowers citizens to demand an economic policy that provides prosperity and opportunity for all. The institute publishes *The EPI Journal*, as well as briefing papers, issue briefs, policy memoranda, and issue guides such as *Minimum Wage, Poverty and Family Budgets*, and *Welfare.*

FreedomWorks

601 Pennsylvania Avenue, NW, North Building, Suite 700
Washington, DC   20004
(202) 783-3870 • fax: (202) 942-7649
Web site: www.freedomworks.org

FreedomWorks is an organization committed to lower taxes, smaller government, and greater freedoms for American citizens. It works toward these goals by training and mobilizing activists and lobbying policy makers. FreedomWorks publishes regular press releases and action alerts.

The Heritage Foundation

214 Massachusetts Avenue NE, Washington, DC   20002
(202) 546-4400 • fax: (202) 546-8328
Web site: www.heritage.org

The Heritage Foundation is a public-policy think tank with emphases on individual liberty, free enterprise, limited government, a strong national defense, and traditional values. It provides information and research on such issues and promotes policy. Its publications include *WebMemos, Backgrounders*, and the *Heritage Hotsheet*, among others.

Internal Revenue Service (IRS)

1111 Constitution Avenue NW, Washington, DC   20224

(800) 829-1040
Web site: www.irs.gov

The IRS is a bureau within the U.S. Treasury that facilitates and enforces citizens' compliance with U.S. tax law. It also provides information about compliance to federal, state, and local governments. The IRS publishes fact sheets, research bulletins, and annual data books.

International Monetary Fund (IMF)
700 19th Street NW, Washington, DC   20431
(202) 623-7000 • fax: (202) 623-4661
Web site: www.imf.org

The IMF is an international organization established to promote international monetary cooperation and trade, exchange stability, and economic growth, and to provide temporary assistance to member countries. To accomplish these goals, it monitors economic and financial developments, providing technical and financial assistance, and conducting research. The IMF's publications include the *World Economic Outlook*, the *Global Financial Stability Report*, several periodicals including *IMF Survey* and *IMF Research Bulletin*, and numerous others.

The Tax Foundation
2001 L Street NW, Suite 1050, Washington, DC   20036
(202) 464-6200 • fax: (202) 464-6201
e-mail: tf@taxfoundation.org
Web site: www.taxfoundation.org

The Tax Foundation is a nonpartisan tax research organization that educates taxpayers about tax policy and the current tax burden. It promotes a tax policy that is simple, transparent, stable, neutral, and that promotes growth. The foundation publishes *Fiscal Facts*, the *Tax Watch* and *Tax Features* newsletters, books such as *A Taxpayer's Guide to Federal Spending*, and many others.

Urban Institute

2100 M Street NW, Washington, DC   20037
(202) 833-7200
Web site: www.urbaninstitute.org

The Urban Institute conducts research, analyzes and evaluates policy and programs, and educates citizens with the goal of bringing about effective public policy and government. It focuses on issues of crime and justice, the economy and taxes, health and health care, housing, welfare, and work and income. The Urban Institute Press publishes books such as *Contemporary U.S. Tax Policy* and *War and Taxes*. The institute also publishes commentary, storyboards, and research reports.

U.S. Department of Treasury

1500 Pennsylvania Avenue NW, Washington, DC   20220
(202) 622-2000 • fax: (202) 622-6415
Web site: www.treasury.gov

The U.S. Department of Treasury is the government agency responsible for promoting the nation's economic security and prosperity. The department advises the U.S. president, encourages economic growth, and facilitates the governance of financial institutions. It publishes press releases, fact sheets, and weekly briefings.

Bibliography

Books

Robert D. Atkinson — *Supply-Side Follies: Why Conservative Economics Fails, Liberal Economics Falters, and Innovation Economics Is the Answer*. Lanham, MD: Rowman and Littlefield, 2006.

Neil Boortz and John Linder — *The Fair Tax Book: Saying Goodbye to the Income Tax and the IRS*. New York: Harper, 2006.

Neil Boortz and John Linder — *Fair Tax: The Truth: Answering the Critics*. New York: Harper, 2008.

David Brunori — *Local Tax Policy: A Federalist Perspective*, 2nd ed. Washington, DC: Urban Institute Press, 2007.

David Brunori — *State Tax Policy: A Political Perspective*, 2nd ed. Washington, DC: Urban Institute Press, 2005.

Carmina Y. D'Aversa, ed. — *Tax, Estate, and Lifetime Planning for Minors*. Chicago: American Bar Association, 2006.

John W. Diamond and George R. Zodrow, eds. — *Fundamental Tax Reform: Issues, Choices, and Implications*. Cambridge, MA: MIT Press, 2008.

Robin L. Einhorn — *American Taxation, American Slavery*. Chicago: University of Chicago Press, 2006.

Erich Kirchler *The Economic Psychology of Tax Behaviour*. New York: Cambridge University Press, 2007.

Robert D. Lee Jr., Ronald W. Johnson, and Philip G. Joyce *Public Budgeting Systems*, 8th ed. Sudbury, MA: Jones and Bartlett Publishers, 2008.

J. C. Sharman *Havens in a Storm: The Struggle for Global Tax Regulation*. Ithaca, NY: Cornell University Press, 2006.

Daniel N. Shaviro *Taxes, Spending, and the U.S. Government's March Toward Bankruptcy*. New York: Cambridge University Press, 2007.

Richard G. Sims *School Funding, Taxes, and Economic Growth: An Analysis of the 50 States*. Washington, DC: National Educational Association, 2004.

Joel Slemrod and Jon Bakija *Taxing Ourselves: A Citizen's Guide to the Debate over Taxes*, 4th ed. Cambridge, MA: MIT Press, 2008.

C. Eugene Steuerle *Contemporary U.S. Tax Policy*, 2nd ed. Washington, DC: Urban Institute Press, 2008.

Joseph F. Zimmerman *The Silence of Congress: State Taxation of Interstate Commerce*. Albany: State University of New York Press, 2007.

Periodicals

Gar Alperovitz	"Taking the Offensive on Wealth: Strategies that Unite the Vast Majority Against a Tiny Elite Are Sure to Win," *The Nation*, February 21, 2005.
Edmund L. Andrews	"Death Tax? Double Tax? For Most, It's No Tax," *New York Times*, August 14, 2005.
Edmund L. Andrews	"Hmmm. What's this Alternative Tax? Hey, Wait! Ouch!" *New York Times*, December 4, 2005.
Edmund L. Andrews	"Why U.S. Companies Shouldn't Whine About Taxes," *New York Times*, July 9, 2006.
Anna Bernasek	"'Temporary' Tax Cuts Have a Way of Becoming Permanent," *New York Times*, May 14, 2006.
Michael J. Boskin	"How Not to Fix the Economy," *Wall Street Journal*, December 13, 2007.
John F. Cogan and R. Glenn Hubbard	"The Coming Tax Bomb," *Wall Street Journal*, April 8, 2008.
Clive Crook	"'Starve the Beast' Doesn't Work," *National Journal*, August 11, 2007.
Stephen J. Entin	"Save the Bush Tax Cuts," *Wall Street Journal*, October 19, 2007.
Rodney Everson	"A Bubble-icious Tax Cut," *Barron's*, November 14, 2005.

Steve Forbes	"One Simple Rate," *Wall Street Journal*, August 21, 2005.
Mike Franc	"Recast Federal Entitlements, Fight Tax Hikes," *Human Events*, February 19, 2007.
Mike Franc	"Strengthening Free Enterprise," *Human Events*, January 22, 2007.
Robert H. Frank	"Sometimes, A Tax Cut for the Wealthy Can Hurt the Wealthy," *New York Times*, November 24, 2005.
Robert H. Frank	"Tax Cuts for the Wealthy: Waste More, Want More," *New York Times*, December 22, 2005.
Robert H. Frank	"Why Not Shift the Burden to Big Spenders?" *New York Times*, October 7, 2007.
Jason Furman	"End the Mortgage-Interest Deduction!" *Slate*, November 10, 2005.
James K. Galbraith	"Fair, Not Balanced," *Mother Jones*, July/August 2005.
Jeb Henserling	"AMT Repeal: To Tax or Not to Tax—That Is the Question," *Human Events*, October 18, 2007.
Arlie Hochschild	"The Chauffeur's Dilemma," *The American Prospect*, July 2005.
R. Glenn Hubbard	"The Corporate Tax Myth," *Wall Street Journal*, July 26, 2007.

John S. Irons and John Podesta — "A Tax Plan for Progressives," *American Prospect*, June 2005.

Scott Johnson and John Hinderaker — "Broad Ownership Needs Broad Taxpaying," *American Enterprise*, March 2005.

David Cay Johnston — "If I Were a Rich Man ..." *Sojourners*, April 2005.

Paul Krugman — "The Great Wealth Transfer," *Rolling Stone*, December 14, 2006.

Arthur Laffer and Stephen Moore — "As the World Turns," *American Spectator*, February 2008.

John Maggs — "Fading Away?" *National Journal*, July 28, 2007.

John Maggs — "No Alternatives," *National Journal*, April 14, 2007.

John Maggs — "The Vanishing Taxpayer," *National Journal*, April 22, 2006.

David Malpass — "The Washington Tax Mess," *Forbes*, July 23, 2007.

N. Gregory Mankiw — "The Problem with the Corporate Tax," *New York Times*, June 1, 2008.

Edward F. McQuarrie — "The Unkindest Tax Cut," *Barron's*, September 4, 2006.

Stephen Moore — "The Investment Slowdown," *Wall Street Journal*, February 14, 2008.

Stephen Moore — "The Laffer Curve Strikes Again," *American Spectator*, September 2006.

Stephen Moore   "Reaganomics 2.0," *Wall Street Journal*, August 31, 2007.

Stephen Moore   "Real Tax Cuts Have Curves," *Wall Street Journal*, June 13, 2005.

Stephen Moore   "Supply Side: How to Soak the Rich (the George Bush Way)," *Wall Street Journal*, May 4, 2006.

Stephen Moore   "The Supply-Side Solution," *Wall Street Journal*, November 9, 2007.

Stephen Moore   "Through the Roof!" *Weekly Standard*, December 17, 2007.

New York Times   "The Tax Debate that Isn't," December 13, 2007.

Jonathan Rauch   "Stoking the Beast," *Atlantic*, June 2006.

Uwe Reinhardt   "Stop Those Rebate Checks!" *Modern Healthcare*, February 18, 2008.

Dan Rosenblum   "Carbon: Tax Not Cap-and-Trade," *Tikkun*, July/August 2007.

USA Today   "What's Missing in Tax Talk," December 27, 2007.

Wall Street Journal "Taxes and Income," December 17, 2007.

Eric Wattree   "Selling Gucci Bags in a Homeless Shelter," *Los Angeles Sentinel*, May 18–24, 2006.

Index